WHAT DOES A HOUSE WANT?

ALSO BY GARY GEDDES

Poetry:

- *Poems* (1971)
- *Rivers Inlet* (1972)
- *Snakeroot* (1973)
- *Letter of the Master of Horse* (1973)
- *War & other measures* (1976)
- *The Acid Test* (1980)
- *The Terracotta Army* (1984)
- *Changes of State* (1986)
- *Hong Kong* (1987)
- *No Easy Exit* (1989)
- *Light of Burning Towers* (1990)
- *Girl by the Water* (1994)
- *The Perfect Cold Warrior* (1995)
- *Active Trading: Selected Poems 1970-1995* (1996)
- *Flying Blind* (1998)
- *Skaldance* (2004)
- *Falsework* (2007)
- *Swimming Ginger* (2010)

Fiction:

- *The Unsettling of the West* (1986)

Non-Fiction:

- *Letters from Managua: Meditations on Politics & Art* (1990)
- *Sailing Home: A Journey through Time, Place & Memory* (2001)
- *Kingdom of Ten Thousand Things: An Impossible Journey from Kabul to Chiapas* (2005)
- *Drink the Bitter Root: A Search for Justice and Healing in Africa* (2012)

WHAT DOES A HOUSE WANT?

Selected Poems
by

GARY GEDDES

RED HEN PRESS
Pasadena, CA

Book design by Natasha Castro
Book layout by Rosemary McGuinness
Cover design by Rebecca Buhler

Library of Congress Cataloging-in-Publication Data
Geddes, Gary.
  [Poems. Selections]
  what does a house want? : Selected Poems / by Gary Geddes.—First
Edition.
     pages cm
  Includes bibliographical references and index.
  ISBN 978-1-59709-276-0 (alk. paper)
  I. Title.
  PR9199.3.G4W43 2014
  811'.54—dc23

                    2013030248

The Los Angeles County Arts Commission, the National Endowment for
the Arts, the Pasadena Arts & Cultural Commission and the City of Pasa-
dena Cultural Affairs Division, the Los Angeles Department of Cultural
Affairs, the Dwight Stuart Youth Fund, and Sony Pictures Entertainment
partially support Red Hen Press.

First Edition
Published by Red Hen Press
www.redhen.org

Acknowledgments

I would like to thank all those publishers who have been interested in my poetry over the years: Waterloo Lutheran University Press, Talonbooks, House of Anansi, Oberon Press, Turnstone Press, Coteau Books, Oolichan Books, Peterloo Poets, Enitharmon Press, and, especially, Goose Lane Editions for permission to reprint various poems. Among the many friends who have given me critical advice and editorial suggestions over a lifetime, I want to thank Margaret Atwood, Michael Ondaatje, P. K. Page, Earle Birney, Al Purdy, Phyllis Bruce, Jan Jeffers, Ron Smith, John Gilmore, Chris Knight, Harry Chambers, Andrew Mitchell, Stephen Stuart-Smith, Doug Isaac, Ross Leckie, Jim Anderson, Hal Wake, and friends at CBC and BBC radio. Among the granting agencies that have provided financial assistance over a lifetime, I am pleased to acknowledge Canada Council for the Arts, Ontario Arts Council, the Department of Foreign Affairs, and the BC Arts Council. Without the moral support of family, friends, colleagues, and sympathetic reviewers, my task would have been more difficult and considerably less enjoyable.

Special thanks to Martin Honisch for use of his painting, *Mon Cheval*, for the front cover art of this book.

for Ann

TABLE OF CONTENTS

WHAT DOES A HOUSE WANT?

ONE

It takes so little, so infinitely little, for a person to cross the border beyond which everything loses meaning: love, conviction, faith, history. Human life—and herein lies the secret—takes place in the immediate proximity of that border, even in direct contact with it; it is not miles away, but a fraction of an inch.

—Milan Kundera

TOWER

I loved them, in my own way,
enough to pay hard cash for the rifle,
to plan my strategy long into the night.
I did not complain about the cold wind
or the exhausting climb to the tower;
even the long wait and the rank-smelling
pigeons never taxed my patience.

When they emerged, after a time,
into the bright winter sun at mid-day,
I spared no effort to steady the rifle,
to bring the delicate cross of the gun-sights
into line with their temples or breasts.

And when they began to run, after the first
had settled to rest in the soft snow,
I never lost my cool, but took them
one by one, like a cat collecting kittens.

SANDRA LEE SCHEUER

—Killed at Kent State University, May 4, 1970
by the Ohio National Guard.

You might have met her on a Saturday night,
cutting precise circles, clockwise, at the Moon-Glo
Roller Rink, or walking with quick step

between the campus and a green two-story house,
where the room was always tidy, the bed made,
the books in confraternity on the shelves.

She did not throw stones, major in philosophy
or set fire to buildings, though acquaintances say
she hated war, had heard of Cambodia.

In truth she wore a modicum of make-up, a brassiere,
and could no doubt more easily have married a guardsman
than cursed or put a flower in his rifle barrel.

While the armouries burned, she studied,
bent low over notes, speech therapy books, pages
open at sections on impairment, physiology.

And while they milled and shouted on the commons,
she helped a boy named Billy with his lisp, saying
Hiss, Billy, like a snake. That's it, SSSSSSSS,

tongue well up and back behind your teeth.
Now buzz, Billy, like a bee. Feel the air
vibrating in my windpipe as I breathe?

As she walked in sunlight through the parking-lot
at noon, feeling the world a passing lovely place,
a young guardsman, who had his sights on her,

was going down on one knee, as if he might propose.
His declaration, unmistakable, articulate,
flowered within her, passed through her neck,

severed her trachea, taking her breath away.
Now who will burn the midnight oil for Billy,
ensure the perilous freedom of his speech;

and who will see her skating at the Moon-Glo
Roller Rink, the eight small wooden wheels
making their countless revolutions on the floor?

PROMISED LAND

When I went to spy out the land
I took shin pads, gas mask,
snow tires with metal studs, radar,
bazookas, reconnaissance planes,
foot powder, dental floss, FN
rifles, forged passport, a dozen
languages, hospital insurance,
and a jock-strap with a metal cup.

On my way to case the land
I took Batman comics, walkie-talkie,
hand-grenades and bayonets, a yoyo,
the memory of mother waving clean socks
and underwear, life insurance,
the *Encyclopaedia Britannica,* Moses's
blessing, a cassette, a mickey of rye,
anti-histamine, a few addresses,
bongo drums, *Playboy,* equipment
for wire-taps, green garbage bags,
Kleenex, laxative, an inflatable raft,
pemmican, flares, corn-plasters,
return tickets, spare batteries,
contraceptives, an atlas.

I knew this was the right place,
I sold the whole lot the first day.

YEAR OF THE CHILD

What did it matter, after all,
that we were careful with matches,
never dined on sleeping-pills or Drano,
turned down candy and rides
even from the next-door neighbor
who was old, religious, and (we thought) harmless,
kept our pencil-sharpened fingers out of sockets,
did not eat geraniums or dieffenbachia,
looked both ways for traffic
before crossing the street like somnambulists
with both arms extended,
didn't defy gravity or try to breathe underwater,
never stuck our tongues out at passing motorists
lest they be members of the Mafia on holiday,
said our prayers frequently if without fervour,
opened infant bank accounts, allowed insurance
to be taken out in our names for college,
never testified in court against our parents
or appealed the Bill of Rights.
When the time came, they hired killers
to baby-sit, glared at us
along gun-barrels, tossed us from windows,
doctored the Kool-Aid, set us adrift
in colanders (we mistook the mines
for bull-rushes), our burst eardrums
deaf to the strains of Brahms's Lullaby.
What did it matter, after all?
The man who pushed the button
resembled Hans Christian Andersen.

Word

I became flesh;
I swam, impatient,
in placental waters.

Rubber gloves
guided my lethal skull
into the breach, launched me
into thinner seas.

A quart of good champagne
splashed down my sides,
a tiny motor
propelled me forward.

Ship after ship went
down, the screams
of men meant nothing.
I sang in the air,
my song
shattered a child's thought.

They planted me in fields,
under bridges, no one
collected the pieces.
They dropped me on cities;
the charred flesh stuck
in my throat.

They updated me, made me
streamlined, beautiful.
I grew vain. My lust
could not be glutted.
I turned on them.

They spoke of god, of honor.
I wiped my mouth
on my sleeve.

THE ANIMALS

We began as dark eyes
in dark places,
reluctant to keep
appointments.

A shape emerged
from the shadowy poplars,
pumping action of knees
in deep snow, rifle
sloped casually down
across a forearm
and dragging something
behind, something dead
to put in a poem.

No names were given, then,
to what we saw.

So we retreated
further into ourselves,
our disguises, until
we were only words
pitched for oblivion.

Our dust settles
in the space between walls.

The Plants

We considered ourselves
stable, down-to-earth.
No appreciable transience,
though we had our share
of social climbers.

We were what we were,
could always be counted on
to stay in one spot
and produce, or reproduce.

Our politics were conservative:
neither greedy nor revolting,
only dull. What happened?
Was it ambition or vanity,
flying too near the sun
as if to shake off
this labyrinth of roots,
the stigma of place?

Anyway, we got burned.
There was an explosion,
a blinding light.
Our transmitters fritzed,
then melted. A rift
opened in the firmament
and with us went
everything that is.

Time Out for Coca-Cola

Marlon Mendizabel turns on the TV
after a hard day of bargaining. Children
play at his feet, a football match in progress
on the American channel. All morning

he has met with officials at the Coca-Cola
plant, trying to resolve the strike. The Company
has hired three new army officers to direct
warehousing, personnel, and security.

Six eyes want him gone, six new laser eyes
negotiate his disappearance piece
by piece. First his voice, venturing out
passionately, logically, vanishes, as

nothing he says makes the least impression.
Then his hands, picking up the argument,
running interference for his voice, falter,
are brought down short of the goal.

Soon the only arms he has to surrender
are gone too. He leans back, an invisible
man, a *desaparecido*, but the family
hasn't noticed. Nothing done or said

could make him lose face, but that went too
along with the rest. He's not alone.
Twenty-seven union leaders
from the National Confederation of Labour

have been kidnapped; two months later
another seventeen, murders confirmed
by the Conference of Guatemalan Bishops.
Marlon wants to live for the sake of his kids,

but it's too late. Of the 208 bones in his body,
half have returned to the packing-crates.
His abdomen shrinks from its diet of fear.
His children watch the soft drink commercial

on television, cheering on the Coke truck
as it falls behind that of its rival. He wants
to tell them it's a matter of ethics, not taste,
that the truck contains the bones of 100,000

murdered Guatemalans, killed by death-squads
in the pay of government and large corporations.
Instead, he lays an invisible hand on their heads
and offers up a silent prayer for their safety.

Marlon's heart grows so large it fills the room
until even those on television notice
and stop what they're doing to watch and listen
to the message of that heart as it communes

with God. Football players take off helmets
and stand with heads bowed; the announcers,
for once, are at a loss for words. Outside
Dallas, the Coke truck pulls over, lights

flashing. A door opens and those bones
form a vast bridge that stretches all the way
to Guatemala City. Children are crossing, hands
joined, singing. Nothing can stop them.

Letter of the
Master of Horse

I was signed
on the King's authority
as master of horse.
Three days
                    (I remember
                    quite clearly)
three days after we parted.
I did not really believe it,
it seemed so much the unrolling
of an incredible dream.

                    *

Bright plumes, scarlet tunics,
glint of sunlight on armour.
Fifty of the King's best horses,
strong, high-spirited, rearing
to the blast of trumpets,
galloping
down the long avenida
to the waiting ships.
And me, your gangling brother,
permitted to ride with cavalry.

                    *

Laughter,
children singing
in the market, women

dancing, throwing flowers,
the whole street covered
with flowers.
In the plaza del sol
a blind beggar kissed my eyes.
I hadn't expected the softness
of his fingers
                moving upon my face.

                ★

A bad beginning.
The animals knew, hesitated
at the ramps, backed off,
finally had to be blindfolded
and beaten aboard.

Sailors grumbled for days
as if we had brought on board
a cargo of women.

                ★

But the sea smiled.
Smiled as we passed
through the world's gate,
smiled as we lost our escort
of gulls. I have seen
such smiles on faces of whores
in Barcelona.

*

For months now
an unwelcome guest
in my own body.
I squat by the fire
in a silence broken only
by the tireless grinding
of insects.
I have taken
to drawing your face
in the brown earth
at my feet

         (The ears are
         never quite right).

*

You are waving,
waving. Your
tears are a river
that swells, rushes beside me.

I lie for days
in a sea drier than the desert
of the Moors
but your tears are lost,
sucked
into the parched throat of the sky.

*

I am watched daily.
The ship's carpenter is at work
nearby, within the stockade,
fashioning a harness for me
a wooden collar. He is a fool
who takes no pride in his work,
yet the chips lie about his feet,
beautiful as yellow petals.

*

Days melt
in the hot sun, flow
together. An order is given
to jettison the horses,
it sweeps like a breeze
over parched black faces.

*

I am not consulted, though
Ortega comes to me later
when it is over and says:

> God knows, there are men
> I'd have worried less to lose.

*

The sailors are relieved,
fall to it with abandon.
The first horse is blindfolded,
led to the gunwales, and struck
so hard it leaps skyward
in an arc, its great body
etched against the sun.

I remember thinking
how graceless it looked,
out of its element, legs
braced and stiffened
for the plunge.

*

They drink long
draughts, muzzles submerged
to the eyes, set out like spokes
in all directions.
The salt does its work.
First scream, proud head
thrown back, nostrils flared,
flesh tight over teeth
and gums

                    (yellow teeth,
                    bloody gums).

The spasms, heaving bodies,
turning, turning.
I am the centre
of this churning circumference.
The wretch beside me,
fingers
knotted to the gunwales.

*

They plunge toward
the ship, hooves crashing
on the planked hull.
Soft muzzles ripped
and bleeding on splintered wood
and barnacles.
The ensign's mare
struggles half out of the water
on the backs of two
hapless animals.

*

When the affair ended
the sea was littered with bodies,
smooth bloated carcasses.
Neither pike pole nor ship's
boats could keep them off.

Sailors that never missed
a meal retched violently
in the hot sun. Only
the silent industry of sharks
could give them rest.

*

What is the shape of freedom,
after all? Did I come here
to be devoured by insects, or
maddened by screams in the night?
Ortega, when we found him,
pinned and swinging in his bones,
jawbone pinned and singing
in the wind: God's lieutenant,
more eloquent in death.

*

Sooner or later hope
evaporates, joy itself
is seasonal. The others?

They are Spaniards, no more
and no less, and burn with a lust
that sends them tilting
at the sun itself.

Ortega, listen, the horses,
where are the sun's horses
to pull his chariot from the sea,
end this conspiracy of dark?

The nights are long, the cold
a maggot boarding in my flesh.

★

I hear them moving,
barely perceptible, faint
as the roar of insects.
Gathering,
gathering to thunder
across the hidden valleys
of the sea, crash of hooves
upon my door, hot quick
breath upon my face.

My eyes, he kissed my eyes,
the softness of his fingers
moving . . .

★

Forgive me, I did not
mean this to be my final
offering. Sometimes the need

to forgive, be forgiven,
makes the heart a pilgrim.
I am no traveller,
my Christopher faceless
with rubbing on the voyage
out, the voyage into exile.

Islanded in our separate
selves, words are
too frail a bridge.

⋆

I see you in the morning
running to meet me down
the mountainside, your face
transfigured with happiness.
Wait for me, my sister,
where wind rubs bare
the cliff face, where we rode
to watch the passing ships
at day break, and saw them
burn golden, from masthead
down to waterline.

⋆

I will come soon.

Two

Poetry makes language care because it renders everything intimate.... There is nothing more substantial to place against the cruelty and indifference of the world than this caring.

—John Berger

The Strap

No other sound was heard throughout the school
as Jimmy Bunn surrendered to the strap.
He stood before me in the counsellor's office
eye to eye, while the desk drawer gaped,
his farmer's hands stretched out in turn
expectant as beggars. My heart was touched.
I gave them more than they had bargained for.
Six on each. The welts, like coins,
inflated as we watched. Nothing he'd done
deserved such largesse, disrupting my sermon
on the Bay of Pigs invasion and how Americans
are hooked on violence, etcetera, etcetera.
They say there's a kinship in aggression
that knits the torturer and his victim;
we came to be the best of friends.
But each excuse and subterfuge exploded
in my brain as he dropped his puffed pink hams
and fought back tears. I put the leather tongue
into the gaping drawer and pushed it shut.

Jimmy's Place

We found the cow in a grove below the road,
leaning against an alder for support,
her udder swollen, her breath ragged and grating
as a rasp. I could have drowned
in the liquid eye she turned to me.
Her calf, though dead, was perfectly positioned,
forelegs and head protruding from the flaming ring
of vulva. Too large, perhaps, or hind legs
broken through the sac, dispersing fluids.
Much as we tried we couldn't pry it loose
and the flesh around the legs began to give
from pressure on the rope. The cow
had no more strength and staggered back
each time we pulled. Tie her to the tree,
I said, being the schoolmaster and thinking
myself obliged to have an answer, even here
on the High Road, five miles south of town
where the island bunched in the jumble
of its origins. It was coming, by God,
I swear it, this scrub roan with her shadow self
extending out behind, going in both directions
like a '52 Studebaker, coming by inches
and our feet slipping in the mud and shit
and wet grass. She raised her head and tried
to see what madness we'd concocted in her wake,
emitted a tearing gunny-sack groan,
and her liquid eye ebbed back to perfect white.

HIGH GROUND

Submerged beneath three feet of snow
my neighbor's boat serves notice
of an option set aside. He's not a neighbor,
not exactly, owns but does not live

on fifty acres severed from the parcel
that contained my land. He planned
a house for his retirement, the baleful boat
an emerald to adorn his fantasy. It sits

on high ground near the unused sugar shack,
host to small animals, inscribed with memories
of a flood, an inland ocean lapping struts
and ribs. They winter déclassé in this scuttled

ark. The trailer rusts, the mast has grown
a beard of moss. Receding waters took their time
to carve the fossils in my patio, unlike
the splitting fibreglass near Archie's keel.

SASKATCHEWAN: 1949

Father is riding
the ridgepole of the new barn
and dreaming ocean.

He grips the keel
with shipwright's thighs.
Studs and two-by-fours
like bleached, white ribs
take measure of the sky.

He cannot fathom the wash
of tides, war's currents,
love's coups d'état,
that ground him
on this ancient seabed
of prairie.
          He knows
what his fingers know:
claw hammer, crowbar,
and a clutch of nails.

Close-hauled bed sheets
nudge the house to windward.
Ripe wheat breaks like surf
on beaches of new lumber.

Ahoy! Ahoy! cries Noah
from his ark.

Shoals of brown cattle
dot the sweet-grass shallows.
Crows swim up like sturgeon
from the startled corn.

SUBSIDIES

A boy with a mechanical arm
addresses a group of kids
on farm safety;
a farmer tries to talk
to the camera—still asking himself
how it happened—youngest son, beside him
one moment on the fender,
slipping under the rear wheel of the tractor.

Eighty percent of rural deaths,
the voice explains,
are the result of farm accidents.

Statistics are no consolation
when you've seen the support-block
give way and the circular saw
walk through the flesh of your son's neck.
At night as you drift towards sleep
you see the recognition
in his startled eyes;
cock's crow
is the engine's whine.

A year later, you still can't look at her
over breakfast, rise
to the need in her flesh
or yours. You toy with an egg,
hard-boiled and intransigent
on your plate, invite
the coffee to burn your lips.

You hear them debate subsidies
in parliament, the future of the family farm,
and you know that nothing you plant
will ever again grow straight,
nothing you do
will ever make it right.

HOMEWORK

As I turn the car up the driveway,
I can see my Jan in the rear-view mirror
dragging Mac and the four cats, all dead,
on a toboggan over the hill to the first field.

We couldn't bear to see him suffer a winter
of isolation in the barn as rabies
sowed havoc in his blood, this haywire
border collie whose speed carried him

up the trunk of the maple, where he'd bite
the first branch and drop eight feet
to the ground, the breed too high-strung
for easy domesticity or the safety

of small children. I held him in my arms
while the vet injected a fatal solution into his veins.
A slight quiver as the heart and other organs
registered shock and he was gone,

all that neurotic energy reduced to mere weight
and the damp nose going dry as I chalked up
another F as care giver. I roll the window
down to wave, but Jan doesn't notice, her body

bent to the terrible task, chipping away
at the frozen ground with the new spade
from Canadian Tire. I re-check my briefcase
and the bundle of unmarked essays

on the back seat, depress the accelerator,
and ease gas into the humming cylinders.
Wheels spin in the loose gravel, then the car
leaps forward onto the paved road.

GROUSE

Each day, the grouse explodes
at a certain juncture in the cedars,
beating a quick departure
through the lower branches.

If I forget, the sudden movement
startles me; more often, though,
I hold my breath and try to guess
the exact spot, exact moment

of lift-off. Experience tells me
there's a nest nearby, the frantic
exit just a ploy to put me off
the track; the hound, as well, whose

shortcut intersects the perilous
flight path of the grouse. I know
the dolour of the empty nest. My mother,
half a century dead, pushes north

along Commercial Drive a pram.
She faces a mountain bearing the name
of the bird my passage has dislodged,
smiles at the mewling infant self

I can't imagine. My father, startled,
beats his own retreat in wartime,
drums for wings. Distraction
works as well as lethal talons

if the intruder proves disinterested,
inept. A scent has caught the dog's
attention. As for me, I read the signs,
briefly pause to urinate, push on.

The Quality of Light

The quality of light is what arrests the man
moving by gradations through the snowy field
on skis. He eyes the outlines of trail broken yesterday,
shaped and contoured by wind, wind that never
sleeps yet seldom tires of letting its cold tongue

sculpt and sweep a tentative world of forms.
Two steps behind, conserving energy by keeping
to the beaten track, the dog takes bites of snow
and contemplates an archaeology of smell:
spoors, markings of its undomesticated kind

that cross this man-made path at random,
making their own incursions in the narrative.
As the sun's rays, denied by angle and position
of the Earth their customary part, ricochet
a thousand times among the mirrored crystals,

emerging more intense than light itself, so the man
stumbles from thought to thought, a blinking
newborn Lazarus. Sculpted troughs, too narrow
now for use, bind harnesses together, or nudge
one tip across another for a fall. The dog looks on,

one could say amused, though not itself sure-footed
on this stage. Man and dog recall how February
storms cause dunes of snow to curl like breaking
waves. Imagine them explorers in Sahara, grit
of sand in mouth, eyes asquint against abrasion.

Flesh dreams water, requires protection from sun
that burns whatever peeks from hair or cloth. Light
there is thick and granular and radiates in ridges
from the ground. Here the man with bamboo poles
extending from his arms learns to cover space

by watching his companion, reaching back in time
to when four limbs propelled him. The rigid sticks
beneath his feet are diverging lines in a parallel
universe of cold, where he pauses, almost snow-blind,
old, and thinks of history every day rewritten,

revisionist monks, amnesiac ideologues in flowing
robes, sees them near stone fences fast at work,
pretends scant notice and, ploughing his way
through a no-man's-land of ice, records
the wins and losses on both sides.

THREE

Poetry is mortal breath that
knows it's mortal.

—Robert Hass

Philip Larkin

He was a man whose words stopped short
of ecstasy, whose impaired tongue and ear refused
the grand theme, the gesture of extravagance,
and found, instead, out along the side-roads,

pant-leg rolled, cycle propped against a tree,
a desperation so quietly profound even Toad,
blinking among grass-spears, had overlooked.
He composed no score for happiness, but improvised

a life of common pleasures taken in a minor key:
a few pints with friends who didn't talk of poetry,
an early morning stroll in Pearson Park,
industrialists' gift to dreary, fog-bound Hull,

sausages on campus, a slice of Humber pie.
Hearing-aid turned off, he tunes his inner music,
private soul station, some such jazz,
communes with Jelly Roll and Beiderbecke,

and watches from his window at the Nuffield,
where Westbourne intersects with Salisbury,
winos rub themselves against the freshly painted
thighs of mermaids in the Victorian fountain,

who take their own libations from a conch.
While such doleful enthusiasts drink his health,
all flesh conspires to silence Larkin;
he undergoes a sea-change in the Avenues.

With no more reason to attend, he sings the poem
of his departure, achieves his wish to be alone.
Propped up in bed and talking to himself,
one thing only is denied: the desire of oblivion.

Mahatma Gandhi Refuses an Invitation to Write for *Reader's Digest*

Gentlemen:

celibacy, in the extreme,
is no less violent
than sex

blood is thicker
than the briny, clichéd waters
of Chowpatty Beach
but religion will prove
thicker than both

a man's life
cannot be condensed
to a series of major scenes
in lighted boxes
without distortion

nor did the letter of an obscure
Indian lawyer
secure the release
of Sacco & Vanzetti

Tagore, as he sits beside me
in the wicker armchair,
waiting to be photographed,
appears massive, twice my size,
yet there's no denying
the delicacy and grace

of the manuscript
he holds awkwardly in his lap
or the confidence
he has given the people
in their roots

the dead woman in the street
outside the railway station
in Bombay is not there
to provoke the curiosity
or guilt of tourists

there are wounds
no amount of salt can heal
regardless of the manufacturer

Indigestibly yours

THE LAST CANTO

I seldom budge
from Rapallo.
Venice is no Byzantium
these final days.
Stench from the canals
worse than the cattle ship
I sailed to Europe on.

Mr. Nixon was half-right:
poetry did not pay,
but there was a future in it.
The age demanded
a scapegoat and a saint.
Being American
I applied for both jobs.

The world has been my whale-road,
wanderer and seafarer
among the lost manuscripts,
charting connections
few had even dreamed of.
I've gone about my business
like a pack rat.
You have to do that,
have on hand ten times
what you can ever hope to use.
Tennyson was right
about being part of all he met,
but he hadn't met enough.

As the range broadened
my speech became barbarous,
that of a man who's lost contact
with the words of his fellows,
though he knows their hearts'
most intimate desires.

I once advised trashing the metronome
and composing with the music
of the speaking voice.
Now I say:
Exercise the mind
and school the heart;
voice will rejoice
in its tender chains
like a bridegroom.

While my former countrymen
have given up on ideas,
except in things,
whatever that means,
and play with themselves
like clergymen,
less out of need than habit,
I dream
of ideas in action
and of forma, even the canto,
where the dance of ear
and intellect

draw dormant filings
into the pattern of a rose.

I wrote in an article
in *T.P.'s Weekly* in 1913:
The artist is always beginning.
Any work of art
which is not a beginning,
an invention, a discovery,
is of little worth.

I still hold that view
though at times, I admit,
I counted the cost.

I have spoken too much of usury,
or not enough.
Even the air we breathe
is rented for a price.

Forget my dicta:
direct treatment of the thing
and all that rot.
The thing, so-called,
has yet to be revealed.
I have found poems
to be wiser and more honest
than poets.

Remember the ideogram
from the Chinese,
the one representing truth
which shows a man
standing beside his word.
Nothing more.

The merchant's wife
dying alone
in her unkempt garden
by the river
praises
my irregular feet,
though she draws the line
at Social Credit.

Forget me too:
listen to the poems.

You see, I'm prescriptive
to the end, a weakness
acquired in Hailey, Idaho
and never shaken.

Reading Akio Chida's Translations of the Poems of Toshiko Takada on the Train from Hiroshima to Yokohama

She understood the sisterhood
of suffering and saw the Band-Aid
on a boy in Paris as a badge
of honor.
                    Her finest discriminations
were made on rainy days
under an umbrella.
Comfort of a dead mother's
thin gray hands, faint unreal goodbyes
of those who've yet to learn
what the word signifies.

Melancholy inspired by desert heat
and a donkey, time passing as it does
outside the train window,
mists of Okayama, brown tile roofs
streaking past to disappear
in the dark of tunnels.

                    Poems
so transparent you can feel the ghosts
of children pass through them,
children you might have seen approaching
the bank building where the man
left his shadow forever
on the stone steps, or skipping
along the T-shape of the Aioi Bridge
that morning as the sun withdrew its savings
from the dazzling waters.

THE PRIZE

What we don't need, the faces seem to say,
is another tourist with aching heart
and counterweights for feet. I inch past
twisted girders, photographic
evidence and charred relics of the A-bomb
exhibit, then leave to place a salmon-colored rose
on the monument to Sadako. Six hundred
and forty-four folded paper cranes
did not protect her from white cells
warring in her blood.

Light moves through the exposed
struts of the shattered Dome.
A young girl reads a novel by the river
where a string of rental boats fan out
in the confused current. I can't stop thinking
of Akiko Sato, who died nursing her infant
and left nothing but a slip bearing marks
of black rain. Or the boy survived
only by a metal clasp and scrap of leather
on a pedestal. The Japanese character
embossed on Akira Sakanoue's belt buckle
resembles a beetle. I carry my rough approximation
back through the gleaming downtown,
where shops are full of Italian silks
and the pedestrian crosswalks are playing
a computerized version of "Coming Through the Rye."

The clerk at the hotel smiles at my calligraphy
and draws the correct version in an upright position

in the margins of my notebook. *Shou,*
she pronounces. But what does it mean,
I ask, knowing the two characters for the city,
hiro and *shima,* mean broad island. She's
as efficient as she is beautiful, flesh and bones
so palpably there beneath the immaculate folds
of the uniform. *If a body kiss a body,*
need a body cry. She checks her dictionary,
smiles again. Just as I thought,
she says, turning the open pages towards me,
the character, in English, means *prize.*

O, Akira, Akiko, I languish in the body
and its fires. If I were a Buddhist,
I'd say, without hesitation, show me the road
that leads beyond desire, or
settle for silence. But I see a desperate
paper-wager, a young mother
yearning to give suck, and a boy
so anxious to serve in the Emperor's
demolition squad—belt buckle
shined, kamikaze of the dust brigade—
he scrubs his small round face until it hurts.

One word after another, reaching out
unstable as molecules, able to take
just so much heat. A spit
of moisture whistles
briefly in the kiln,
is gone.

THE TERRACOTTA ARMY

CHARIOTEER

So they call you layabouts a standing army?
There's more life in this terracotta nag

than in the whole first division. With that
Bi leapt on the back of a cavalry pony he had fired

the previous day and dug his heels into the outline
of ribs. I wouldn't have been surprised

to see it leap into action and clear the doorway
with the potter shouting death to the enemy.

Most of the animals were cast from a single mould
and could be distinguished one from the other

only by the application of paint and dyes. I took
exception to this and remarked that, as charioteer,

I found more distinctive characteristics in horses
than in men. Bi swung his legs over the neck

and dropped to the ground. He was no taller
than the ponies he fashioned. Then, with a flourish,

he drew a green moustache on the horse's muzzle
and fell about the pottery amused by his own joke.

Spearman

Before double-ninth day, my measure was taken
in a single sitting, so sure were Lao Bi's

eye and hand. The tenth month I returned
with armoured vest and spear and struck a pose

that pleased him so much he laughed out loud
and threw his wineskin at my feet.

He called me the youngest of the Immortals
and promised me a place in the glory-line.

The likeness was uncanny, not just the face,
but the way the sleeves bunched up at the wrists,

studs and fluted leather of the shoulder-pads.
I was drawn to it again and again as if by magic.

One day, without warning, we left for the frontier
and I felt a greater reluctance

to part with this pottery replica of myself
than I had in taking leave of my own village.

Bi used to slap me on the back and say,
you're too serious to be a soldier.

GUARDSMAN

At first I did not like him and put it down
to the arrogance of the creative mind,

his not mine. I'd been the previous day,
guarding the entrance to Ch'in Shi Haung's tomb,

where the artisans and craftsmen were at work
fashioning god knows what final luxuries

for the imperial afterlife. By the sounds of it,
they were feeling no pain. I mentioned this

quite casually, by way of small talk,
to the master potter as he examined my skull

and he exploded like a devil, threatening
to cut off my head for more detailed study.

Needless to say, I wasted no time absenting myself
from his presence and stopped in for a drink

at my quarters. They told me the tomb was finished
and the great door had been dropped into place,

sealing in every artist and workman employed there.
My hands flew, of their own accord, to cover my throat.

MINISTER OF WAR

I was a young man on the make, a brain for hire,
a travelling politician. I saw my chance,

adopted Ch'in, advised the death of feudal tenure,
not to mention purges and the burning of books.

I scorned the golden mean of men like Mencius
and learned my politics from rats in the latrine;

yet I had respect enough for the written word to know
that old records and systems are better destroyed

than left to seed rebellion and discontent in the period
of transition. The same logic applied to scholars

and authors, those masters of anamnesis, or recall.
I kept the Emperor occupied with toy soldiers

and the arts, or fears of death and court intrigue,
while the real politics unfolded as I knew it would:

highways, taxes, centralization, promotion by exam.
He might have stopped my war against the past,

but I saw to the depths of his and all men's hearts,
where artist lies down, at last, with bureaucrat.

LIEUTENANT

You might call me a jack-of-all-the-arts;
I paint, draw maps, sing, write a fair poem.

I skipped basic training because of the length
of my tongue and managed to nab a commission

right away in the reserve. I can toss off a lyric
or forge an epic in a single afternoon,

still observing the unities. Once I entered
the Emperor's competition and almost made it

to the finals. As far as visual arts are concerned,
I'm no slouch either. I've been known to sketch

enemy encampments in pitch black, still mounted,
give an accurate impression of slaughter

on the battlefield, avoiding dangerous skirmishes
and ignoring cries for help in order to complete

my precious record. The potter was not impressed.
Learn to write with this, he said, positioning

my hands on the jade hilt of an ornate sword,
the enemy has not yet learned to read.

PAYMASTER

We stood beside the trenches and looked at the rows
of figures there, bronze horses harnessed in gold

and silver, some of the charioteers in miniature
with robes and hairstyles denoting superior rank;

then the pottery horses with their snaffle bits
and bridles of stone beads. These had been fired

in one piece, except for the tail and forelock.
Most of the men could be seen to wear toques

over their topknots. Kang, of course, had abandoned
such fashions and stood there with an undying leer

and his pot-belly showing through armour, rivets
forever about to pop. A sensualist. I was astounded

as usual by the loving attention to detail and asked Bi
what thoughts this assembled spectacle called up in him.

Counterfeit currency, he said. A life's work
that will never be seen, poems tossed in bonfires.

A poem lives on in the ear, but a single push
will topple all of these.

INFANTRYMAN

We all marvelled at the courage of Ching K'o,
a serious man of letters who loved books

and often drank to excess with dog butchers
and lute players in the market place.

To please the Crown Prince Tan of Yen, who feared
the imminent demise of his kingdom by Ch'in,

Ching K'o agreed to undertake a daring plot
to assassinate the emperor. Delivering the head

of Ch'in's hated enemy, General Fan, in a box,
Ching K'o unrolled a map of the Yen territories

to be ceded. When the concealed dagger appeared
Ching K'o snatched it up and grabbed the sleeve

of the Emperor, but the cloth tore in his hand
and his advantage was lost. Bi laughed

at this turn of events and made some remark
about the advantages of shoddy workmanship.

We tended to ignore his smart-ass comments
and asides, but the irony was not lost on us.

Mess Sergeant

It was not so much the gossip that attracted me
to Bi's pottery, though there was plenty of that:

news of the latest atrocities against the people,
rights and property abolished, heads of children

staring vacantly from terraces, dismembered corpses
turning slowly in the current along the north bank

of the Wei. Rather it was a sort of clearing house,
a confessional, where our greatest fears were exorcised

piecemeal through the barter of objective detail.
I remember the day when word came of the taking

of Yen. Streets ran with the color of Ch'in's revenge.
The lute-player, Kao-Chien Li, who had plucked Ching K'o

on his way to assassinate the Emperor, was blinded
and forced to serenade the victors without ceasing,

blood still running down his face and arms.
Not a sound was heard in the pottery, except the crackle

of logs burning and the sizzle of spit as the last
moisture escaped from the baking clay figures.

Military Historian

And so he standardized everything—axes, measures,
even the language itself. Six of this,

six of that, the uniform evils of power.
What can you say about a man who would burn

books and the keepers of books? So great
was his fear of chaos and the unknown

he was a dupe for any kind of mumbo-jumbo
and excess. One of the wily magicians at court

convinced Ch'in he could find the fabled Island
of Immortals, but must take along the price

not only of gold and silver in great abundance,
but also a host of beautiful youths of both sexes.

Ch'in complied. Nothing more was heard of them.
The Emperor put out that they were lost at sea,

but others amongst us presumed the magician
had set himself up nicely on the islands of Fu Sang.

All this came to light much later, when Ch'in
died at the coast, vainly looking out to sea.

BLACKSMITH

Bi remarked on the lethal aspect of the crossbow,
whose trigger mechanism I'd just improved.

Tests had been done that morning on criminal types
who'd failed to comply with laws on standardization.

At short range the crossbow sent a heavy arrow
through the breasts of five men with surprisingly little

loss of speed. It was equally efficient on two others
in full armour, standing back to back outside the gates

of the A-fang palace. I received a rousing cheer
from the assembled soldiers and nobility;

even the castratos pressed into service in the grounds
and gardens seemed more than slightly impressed.

Bi was sweating profusely and I thought he looked
rather pale in the dim light as he worked on details

of the armoured vest of a kneeling crossbowman.
Where is the Dragon, Rain Bringer, Lord of Waters

when we need him, the potter muttered to himself,
wiping the blade of the chisel on his leather apron.

Harness-Maker

The plot to assassinate Ch'in Shi Huang
was a regular topic at the pottery.

Bi used it as an occasion to sound off about one
or other of his pet theories. What did I tell you,

he said one morning, unwrapping the four bridles
I had just delivered, a man who hangs out

with drunkards and ne'er-do-wells can't be all bad, eh?
No wonder his royal highness never sleeps in the same

bed two nights in a row. And his concubines—
what a waste! How can a man with so much on his mind

keep up his standard of performance? I have it
in strictest confidence from the younger sister

of his current favorite that, contrary to legend,
the Dragon of Ch'in is nothing but a worm.

Talk of this sort was confined to a trusted few,
including several peasants who made daily deliveries

of wood and bricks. One, brother of conscript Ch'en She,
squatted like a coiled spring in the corner, grinning.

STRATEGIST

Avoid precipitous cliffs, marshes, quagmires, thickets;
at all times, make the terrain work to your advantage.

Arrive first and lie in wait, rested, fully alert.
Tempt the enemy into the open with shows of weakness.

Don't neglect spies, alliances, the impact of banners, gongs,
drums; detach a flying column, if needed, for a rout.

Better yet, win the war without fighting at all.
Information's the thing. What weapon or scaling device

can replace the trained ear? Nothing, at least
not in my books. There is no sure defense against a good

pair of eyes. The Five Factors remain constant,
and the Five-Year Plans, but what are economies of war

when increased levies exhaust a people's substance
and spirit and bring the aggressor to his knees

before the enemy? Remember, prolonged war is folly;
so, too, is laying siege to a walled city.

Without these principles the whole empire, not just
the imperial army, will be in ruins.

SPY

I'd read Sun Tzu,
that was my mistake,

read his *Art of War*
and committed it to memory.

Li Ssu was impressed; otherwise,
he might have left me alone

tending what few books remained
in the imperial library.

I was without status, no beauty either,
nondescript, down at the heels,

nobody's idea of a good time.
But I had my uses.

I was designated Category Five,
the surviving spy,

and ambled freely between the court
and Bi's establishment,

letting my body go to pot
but not my cover.

COMMANDO

My youngest brother disappeared without a trace
after the first recruitment. He was a musician

of no small promise, had anyone bothered to inquire,
and might have piped the hearts of simple men

to victory or wrapped their deadly wounds in notes
of purest silk. Did he lend his flesh to the rubble

of a wall or make his bones instruments of war?
Don't ask. The new carts rattled by on their standard

axles, half-empty. Next they bred a line of faceless
conscripts. Forced labour and conscription

destroyed the base of agriculture, brought revolt.
Who's to say it wasn't for the best?

You can tell by the lightness of my armour
I'm a crack trooper, trained to take the initiative

in battle. I prayed daily my strength would win
sufficient honor to bring me into the presence

of Ch'in and his bloody Councillor, to strike
a chord that's truly worthy of my brother.

Unarmed Foot-soldier

Education does not win battles or put bread
on the table. I was a student once, I know.

I had my champions, my favorite causes;
afternoons I was not gallivanting in full heat,

I spent debating the meaning of the universe.
Why did I bother? There's nothing quite like war

to clear the head—or remove it. I was drafted,
I became the perfect machine, precision tool

for the mechanics of death. I was programmed
to kill. I did not need spear or crossbow:

a well-placed blow would kill an ox or man
instantly; my special kick was called

the eunuch-maker. Still, my previous studies
were not entirely in vain. I was able to apply

the psychology I'd learned to outwitting the enemy
and, of course, my rivals within the ranks.

The potter read my story to the letter:
poised, unbalanced, deadly hollow.

CAPTAIN OF THE GUARD

Is there no aesthetic consistency anymore,
that's what I want to know.

I registered a complaint, after the first sitting,
that he had taken more time braiding the tail

of a cavalry pony and stippling the sandals
of a kneeling warrior than he had taken

getting the fine detail of this face, which
has turned more than pottery heads in its time.

The next thing I know he's placed the head
of that ugly recruit, now bearded, on the six-foot

frame of an officer and recorded for posterity
my untrimmed growth of whiskers.

No, I don't think it was the booze, at least
not primarily. A man like that creates

his own demons and opiates. Realist or formalist—
choose your poison. Was Ch'in drunk

when he shaved a mountain that thwarted him
and had it painted red, as a warning to all nature?

Unit Commander

I was never too keen about the shape of my ears,
the way they hang there like two horseshoes

someone had stuck on as an afterthought.
So I can't say I was anxious to be duplicated

by this barbarous Southerner, whose words fell
about my feet like shards, kiln-dried and jagged.

We talked at length about Ch'in's appropriations,
not just the women, art, and slaves

acquired from the defeated princes, but also designs
of palaces and gardens ordered to be copied

and reproduced in Hsienyang, as if a man
might live in more than one house at a time.

He raged against the slipperiness of Immortals,
even immortal rats in their underground mazes;

then he went on, too long according to my notes,
about lack of imagination among peoples of the North,

how even into death they must carry a representation
of the living world. I couldn't believe my ears.

QUARTERMASTER

Seize reality in the act,
embrace its opposites like a lover,

without moderation. That's the ticket.
Though the flesh be captive,

insurgent thoughts invade the palace grounds,
storm the reviewing stand. Freedom is born

in the anarchy of spilled blood.
Did I say that, or was it Master Bi?

He spoke so close to my ear as he applied
clay to mould my features that his ideas

invaded my brain as if I were a puppet.
Certainly I don't remember propositions

of that sort ever troubling my professional self,
whose sole task was the dispensing of goods,

not words: weapons, food, clothing, rivets, lumber,
and sundry items for the conduct of war.

And no one ever came to my tent and said:
Hey, buddy, give me a new idea, size five and a half.

Archer

He told me the Emperor's eunuch had paid a visit,
then Ch'in Shi Huang himself, disguised

as a standard bearer. I was half-mad with curiosity
to know what transpired between them. Instead,

I made some joke about the Great Ch'in
apprenticing to a potter. Bi mimed the action

of the crossbow and told me I was on target
as usual. Damn it, he shouted,

the man is hedging his imperial bets!
He knows he'll be judged by the company he keeps,

even underground. I told him I had neither power
nor inclination to fashion a god, simple as that.

Never mind, it's done. He's given me a month
to reconsider, while he swims and scans the seas

for some immortal vessel. Here Bi took my hand
in his terrible grip as if it had been an injured

bird. I felt his breath on my face as he spoke:
A man must know where his destiny lies, eh?

Regimental Drummer

He refused, of course, to acknowledge the likeness
and huffed a good deal when I mentioned it.

I supposed he had a cousin in the imperial guard
but recalled a conversation weeks before

when he'd claimed to have no living relatives.
This is my family now, he'd added, pointing

to several terracotta figures in the corner.
But there wasn't the slightest doubt;

this unarmed soldier, turned slightly to reduce
the target area, legs apart, hands ready to parry

or strike a blow, was none other than Bi himself.
Portrait of the artist as master of martial arts,

in the front line, ready for anything, even his warts
rescued from oblivion. We drank a lot of wine

that night and danced around the pottery, reciting
poems and beating drums for the unsung dead.

A slight smile played around the lips and I found myself
winking at the copy instead of the original.

GENERAL

If this is what we have evolved toward,
I have to laugh. The illusion of full knowledge

gave us a sinister edge. We became the crassest
of materialists and would tolerate neither doubt

nor disturbing hypothesis. In a word, vulgar.
How easily the innocent joy of the enthusiast

gives way to the intolerance of the true believer.
We began, like all the others, with a vision:

unification, call it what you will. The sorcery
of a fixed idea. For this we marched long years,

long miles, until, winning the war, we found we had
lost face. We became the new reactionaries,

eliminating, in short order, all the best minds.
Not everything is dangerous to the body politic.

Being the son of a farmer, I should have remembered
that certain organisms must not only be allowed,

but also actively cultivated. Nature can be studied,
but never controlled or predicted with absolute precision.

MINISTER OF WAR

It's not because of superior rank or position
I'm allotted extra space to speak.

I merely have twice as much to answer for.
I was the right hand of God, responsible

for carrying out the wishes of the Leader.
I grew to be more than a soldier—or less.

A politician, which the potter describes cleverly
as a freak of nature that soars above the crowd

but still has ears close to the ground. Of course
I admired Master Bi. We were inextricably linked

by our humour and intelligence. He spoke in riddles
to confound the wise, but also to spread unrest

among the rank and file. I had plans, my own art
to pursue. I exercised decorum,

arranged for another artist to betray him.
Records were kept, tongues loosed

in the usual ways. The plot, discovered,
required a dénouement.

CHAPLAIN

Someone will break us of the habit of war
by taking away our weapons

and we will march against the darkness
(or will it be light?) naked as newborn babes,

tiny fists opening and closing on nothing.
The only certainty, even under the earth, is change,

whether it be cosmetic, paint flaking away
down the muted centuries, or

something more violent that destroys the form
itself, icons of public and private selves.

With such thoughts I addressed the potter
on more than one occasion, thinking to shock him.

I'd given up the Tao and had even less time
for the ethics of Confucius in the new dispensation.

Rituals and ancestor worship are as useless to soldiers
as scapulimancy and tortoise-shell prophecy.

Only our vanity is monumental, the potter said,
and that, too, can be broken.

Standard Bearer

Who remembers names or issues now?
The wall that taxed us to the limits

stopped neither time nor barbarians.
Birds flew freely over the battlements,

testing the currents of non-aligned air;
so, too, did the arrows of our adversaries.

Then the enemy himself learned to fly
by subtle propaganda into our hearts

or by invention into our very midst,
wreaking havoc like a berserker.

I joined the potter in his rest;
I broke his ranks but could not break his will.

Only our forms endure. And stubborn words
which hover and adhere, attend our passing

like faithful retainers. Remnants
of an age when the mind groped its way

in darkness, without maps of logic or conquest,
sweeping in its wake the relentless dust.

FOUR

In the broken thing, moreover, human agency
is oddly implied: breakage, whatever its cause,
is the dark complement to the act of making.

—Louise Glück

Little Windows

It's difficult now to speak of these things.
I'd rather describe the way light falls
in morning courtyards, on clothes
hung out to dry.
That child in the doorway
turning to the sound of the shutter,
half smiling, half indignant.
And Carmen's hair
filling the entire back window
of the Peugeot.

Fifteen square windows in the Lonquen
poster, a face in all but one.
Campesinos from Isla de Maipo
tortured and buried alive
in lime. Father
and three sons.
Windows of agent
Valenzuela's testimony:
a number killed at the air base,
others thrown into the sea
from helicopters, stomachs opened.

Each poster a small apartment building,
tenants gazing into the street
at some event, a demonstration,
a sunset. Eight more in Valparaiso
who should have looked out on the sea.

I saw bougainvillea
in a restaurant window
near the place of ambush;
and a window with a spiky cactus
in full bloom, a pottery pig
and a string of wicker birds
turning gently in the wind.

Why do they smile, these framed faces,
do they know something we don't?
Behind them perpetual white,
bright light
at the tunnel's end.
Perhaps it is we who are lost
and they looking out at us
from some perfect world,
wondering what all the fuss
is about, why
these masks of suffering.

When they break her eyes
images remain.
Sound of the helicopter
recedes. Sea is a window
above him, water tongues
the red from his stomach.

Human Rights Commission

The small woman seated before you describes her encounters with the military. In advance of the translation you hear the phrase, "Caravan of death." She is not talking about a circus, her husband has not run away to a circus, though one was in town the day you arrived, the real McCoy. Medieval etchings of the Dance of Death flicker in a dark recess of your brain. Do you really want to hear this? Yesterday you were curious, took notes copiously. Numbers, implements of torture, the General who travelled the provinces with his exterminators and a Chihuahua that sat on the back of the car seat licking his ear. October 23, 1973, the end of so much. Five months later she too is arrested, kept naked twenty days, a sack over her head. Kicks, blows, electricity, threats against the children, pretence her husband is still alive. You look again at this woman and wonder how much she is not telling you. A heated pipe. Rats driven into the vagina through a heated pipe. When the interview began, the portable radio was playing "Moon Shadow" by Cat Stevens. A poster on the wall said, in Spanish: "No one disappears into thin air."

MAY DAY

PART ONE

Okay, no story. Cariola Theatre, first of May,
streets empty except for the green armoured vans
known affectionately as butcher shops. Troops
at the ready, in their best Sunday riot gear.
Inside, singing "Adios, General," I can hear
the rock band (half-rhyme with *carnaval*). Oops,
no story. Bass notes massage bone marrow. Any chance
soldiers prefer free verse? I admire the way

they're all on the job. Chicago mentioned, a riot
a hundred years ago, workers killed. The U.S.A.,
how Chileans love it still, the idea. Adrenalin,
body busy shucking its payload of dead skin,
sweat glands working overtime, how the letter "A"
dominates. Hand on the union card, eye on the exit.

PART TWO

Gray canvas worker's gloves mounted
on a slab of wood absorb light
from the slitted windows of the Vicaria.

A grim relic of those for whom Christ,
mounted also on wood, died. Performance
done, burden lifted, he stepped offstage

into the wings of his father's private staff
of angels. Each day, priests pass
families of the disappeared, eyes

averted, minds intent on the larger struggle.
They don't see axe, cart, or broom handle
and a thousand other implements of labour

radiating outwards, though part of them recalls
the words SOMOS MÁS printed underneath.

PART THREE

Yes, numbers count. Together we are more,
a force to be contended with, dumb cattle
driven into stadiums, broken, crushed like ore.
Watch us breed under the earth, battle

forces of darkness, our pit lamps
aglow. Third eyes. Coppery sweat
of our limbs. The General laughs,
but doesn't sleep well: new guards, SWAT,

screened applications. He suspects eucalyptus
of plotting against him. *Casi lo matan*, words
the leaves whisper: headlights bearing down,
screech of tires, gunfire from roadside bushes.

It adds up. Thanksgiving, revenge, woods
alive with birdsong, land no one can own.

Arpilleras

A woman cuts a triangle of corduroy
for a mountain, adjusts the cloth
so it rubs shoulders with another mountain,

candy-striped, and one cut from the sleeve
of a blue school tunic. Behind them
is a second range, probably

near the border in Argentina.
No one asks why distant mountains
are more exotic, with floral designs

from bright curtains, and catch more light,
not the school girls who stand with arms raised
in protest of the municipal order

closing their school, not the old-timers
leaning into death with their white wool hair
and match-stick canes. Her fingers tremble

as she cuts four houses from her husband's
best pair of trousers, worn once
to a christening, once to a union meeting,

and red canvas roofs from the raincoat of a daughter
who left suddenly at night by boat from Valparaiso.
She cross-stitches them to the sackcloth backing

to keep them in place, though she knows
nothing is secure against the night, the rumoured
fires. Tomorrow she will sell

her sackcloth tapestries for milk and beans
to feed the other children, but first
she must dream inhabitants in three dimensions,

the awkward, enduring women, moving
among the plaid windows and paisley shrubbery,
variously dressed, cut from the same cloth.

Dècimas

Carabinero boulevards
in Bellavista, from downtown
to poorest barrios, rundown,
forgotten, God's precious discards.
From armoured trucks the junta guards
dispense their sinister blessings
liberally. We're confessing
to everything: slogans, joy,
love, left-wing thought, fire, scars, the boy
with Carmen Quintana, dressings.

Violeta Parra's clipped lines
will do quite nicely, thank you,
the strict form, repetitions too,
syntactical muscle, no spines
bent in submission. Work refines.
Neruda knew this; so did Yeats.
Power, in general, decimates.
Ten lines, eight syllables in each;
it takes no more than this to reach
the naked heart. Come now, who waits?

This is not a country, he said,
only the draft of a country.
We are all revising, wintry
in our cages, our best dreams wed
to disaster, our best friends dead.
What to do, short of repentance?
Clean the barrel of each sentence,
keep dry the magazine of words.
Be nimble as dancers, goat-herds,
dismantling the barbed-wire fence.

General Cemetery

Between the wrought-iron crosses of the disappeared
are no bored lions, avenues of eucalyptus;
here none go down to corruption

in the splendid isolation of crypt or mausoleum,
where empty skulls imagine their importance
and bones are wont to speak of privilege.

Between the wrought-iron crosses of the disappeared
you'll find no tributes to the intellect,
no verse inscriptions, no trace of Greece or Egypt

in the architecture. Add up the ragged columns
of the dispossessed and let archival winds
record each article of faith.

Between the wrought-iron crosses of the disappeared
only a half-starved dog can pass,
or a hummingbird, his heart in his throat.

He hovers overlong above the opened grave,
bearing witness to travesties
that do not stop with death in Santiago.

A woman's square-heeled shoe protrudes
from heaps of brick and bone, a patch of color
showing through the skein of dust.

Between the wrought-iron crosses of the disappeared
her plastic heels are platforms of dissent;
her wit and candour, crimes against the state.

Place your flower gently now among the nameless dead
and let its beauty fade, its cut throat bleed,
into the silent, unassuming earth.

FIVE

. . . a book should be the axe for the frozen sea within us.

—Franz Kafka

Norwegian Rabbit
(The Trotsky Monologues)

Prologue

Leon Trotsky's final days were spent in Coyoacán, a suburb of Mexico City, where he and his wife Natalia Sedova and entourage were guests at the infamous "Blue House" of Frida Kahlo and Diego Rivera. After an extended period, the Trotskys moved a few blocks away to 45 Calle Viena, where he carried on his writing and political activities against a background of hostility from the pro-Stalin Mexican Communist Party. An attempt, led by Rivera's rival muralist, David Siqueiros, was made on Trotsky's life, during which his American bodyguard, Robert Sheldon Harte, mysteriously disappeared and was later found murdered. Having been deported from Russia, Turkey, France, and Norway, Trotsky was grateful for his Mexican refuge, despite its obvious dangers, and spent his spare time collecting rare cacti, raising chickens and rabbits, and contemplating the fate of the revolution in a world locked in mortal combat. So it was on that fateful morning in August 1940, when he rose early to prepare himself for work on the Lenin biography, several articles, letters to editors, and an appointment to which he had reluctantly agreed.

I

When the Norwegians kicked us out
and we sailed to Mexico in the tanker *Ruth*,
we had icebergs on the starboard side;
on port, the Gulf Stream. I could taste
the continent as we passed
Newfoundland and New England.

Returning from my previous exile the ship
stopped in Halifax, where the circumspect Canadians
wouldn't allow me ashore;
then they arrested the whole family
and held us in detention.
Nothing new in that.

I rise early to feed my rabbits and chickens
in their cages and observe my cacti in the clear light
and cool air of the morning.

Most days I stay bent over my labours
like a monk. Newspapers, essays
commissioned by friends
of Dewey, Breton, and Neibhur,
and the biography of Lenin.
A prisoner of my house,
my convictions.

Then the smells draw me out to Veracruz
or Pátzcuaro. Hills, tender landscapes,
and the blinding light of the Gulf. Picnics,
fishing, always more plants.

When we return from one of these outings
Natalia Sedova begins to tease me. Leon Davidovitch,
she laughs, nature has restored you yet again.
You smile. Your eyes are blue and clear
as the sky. I think, at heart
you're a simple peasant.

Hot and cold, the way winds blow
from the Left. The Spanish phrase for lemming
is *conejo de noruega.*

Norwegian rabbit.

2

Icicles in St. Petersburg, my school friend
Ivan carefully breaking off
the largest and doing his cavalry
charge across the square.

This journey to warmth,
the only snow visible at the rim
of Popo.
                    Gathering cactus
along the dirt roads. How it survives,
hoarding essentials deep inside,
defended by sharp needles,
words that pierce.

This tiny country, rooted
in history: *los indios,*
artists so vibrant and passionate—
those who do not embrace you
and offer refuge rise up
to kill you. Was it loyalty to the Party
or my friendship with Frida
and Diego that prompted Siqueiros

to attack the residence at Calle Viena?
Something about walls. Later,
my protector's body
found discarded, bullet-ridden
in the Desert of the Lions.

By the time we finished
reinforcements, reducing the size
of windows and bricking in
the balcony, my beloved casa
resembled a bunker.

3

Outside, I hear the clucking of my chickens;
in here, the click of the dictating machine
we've nicknamed "Little Joseph."

It's not easy to air in public Stalin's dirty linen,
to admit the revolution was betrayed and sullied
by a bully and psychopath. I told the Dewey
Commission the show trials were a juridical play,
the denouement prepared in advance.

My demand for "permanent revolution" advocates
pruning and renewal to keep the bureaucracy
from promoting privilege.

I've tried to make the point more than once
that Stalin had nothing to do with constructing
the Soviet machine of state; he simply
used it for his own ends.
In his hands, the apparatus grew rigid,
monstrous. I described him
at the time of the October Revolution
as "a gray spot which would sometimes give out
a dim and inconsequential light."

Husbandry is not his strongest suit.

4

The woman writing for *The Tribune* asked me
how it felt to be a hero of the revolution.

She was on assignment in Mexico City
and had large feet protruding
from the kind of hand-made
sandals sold in the Zócalo. The nail
of each big toe was square as a window.

I was shocked. First, by the American-ness
of the query, the blatant interest
in individualist mythology. Second,
by her audacity in thinking I'd actually

answer such a question. I laughed. I could
as easily have chosen anger. Writing
for the Left, she must have expected me
to say the people are the real heroes
of the revolution, that leaders
are mere tentacles grown, or evolved,
to serve the interests of the people.

Instead, I said I felt like Dr. Frankenstein,
who had created a monster that was
out of control. Her turn to pretend
shock at my deviation from the Party line.

She closed her green spiral notebook
and leaned forward. The severity
with which her hair was pulled back
gave her an Asian aspect
and the thickness of the lenses
made her brown eyes even larger
in their narrow envelopes.

You've got it all wrong, she insisted.
The monster was an innocent who never understood
the world's response to him. In the end,
he carried the body of his beloved creator,
who deserted and tried to kill him,
to rest among the ice-floes. You
should be so lucky. I suspect
the truth lies elsewhere.

She pulled one large, unbound, American
foot into her lap and rubbed
the squared nail with her thumb.

5

I should have spent time with my children,
two innocents who waved to me from the crowds
as I was passed overhead toward the exit
of the Modern Circus in Petrograd. So much
pride and pain in their troubled faces:
orphans of ideology.

When I wasn't kept up half the night
addressing the assembled crowd in that building
—workers, cast-offs, infants at their mothers' breasts,
children on shoulders—I was being awakened at five
and taken by tug to talk to the Navy boys
at Kronstadt.

The electric tension of that impassioned human throng,
to quote myself. I chucked my prepared notes
on the floor and was taken over by some extra sense,
an unconscious reserve of empathy that told me
what they needed to hear, the whole crowd
hanging on like that, *infants sucking with their dry lips*
the nipples of revolution.

My opponents picked up the refrain soon enough,
shouting down my speeches or ideas
by saying: "This ain't your Modern Circus."

6

A number of yellow-jackets reconnoitre
the new brickwork. If they're not spying for the GPU
or Siqueiros, they might be seeking refuge
in new ideas. Sylvia's beau Frank Jacson
arrives shortly to show me the second draft
of a confused and indifferent article
about divisions among French Trotskyites.
He should stick to the business
of exports and bring Sylvia instead,
who is helpful and without pretensions.

Avispa, the Spanish for wasp, also means
"sly sort," "wily bird," or in common Mexican usage,
"thief." Waspish, or "quick-tempered,"
de prontos enojos.
Avispero: a wasp's nest, or figure
of speech for the inflammation
know as a carbuncle. Ah yes,
and *Con talle de avispa*:
wasp-waisted.
The Dictionary of American Slang
sent to me from Chicago has twenty-five expressions
to describe an attractive girl.

Yellow-jackets, yellow journalism. I spend
too much time learning languages, acquiring the tools
of wisdom but not the wisdom itself. And what about
the blue-jackets at Kronstadt, so supportive
at first, asking my advice in prison
from their cruiser?

7

Frida and Diego made plans to take me
to the coast, staying in the small village
of Barra de Navidad, where one of his patrons
or hangers-on had provided a beach house
with three rooms and a sprawling veranda,
fully screened. They promised a surprise guest,
but would not divulge his name.

Diego poured tequila while we talked art,
politics, stroganoff. Shadows
played across their glistening faces
with every flicker of the coal-oil wick.
Frida tamped and lit a pipe. Each time
she lifted her thumb from the bowl
it made a sound
like the popping of a small cork.
Several large, gray moths, having reconnoitred
the screened porch, fastened themselves
to the wire gauze. More of my gypsy

relatives, our guest said. Spies,
Diego reiterated. Frida spat,
expelling a strand of tobacco.
A screen test, she replied, *nada más*.
When I asked him about working
with Lang on *The Third Man*, he smiled.
Not me, he said, though I've seen enough
to make my eyes bug-out like that. Diego's
paintings, for example, could transform an eagle
into a hyper-thyroid case.

Edward G. Robinson had driven from Hollywood
in his capacity as art collector. This village,
he confided, is too ramshackle
to be called quaint, but it takes its living
from the sea, not to mention evolutionary relics
like ourselves, we who gather on the seam
of our liberation, or expulsion,
from the source. The question, my dear friends,
is this: Do we come to mourn
or to celebrate?

Mid-morning, he strolled with me,
pant-legs rolled up, taking refuge
in wet sand. His footprints
were half the size of mine. See
how the waves erase them equally,
he sighed. Democracy!

When I spoke of the positive response
my articles received in his country,
Edward G. tossed a flat stone he'd picked up
near the house. It bounced several times
across the water and disappeared
into the curl of a wave. Paint or tar,
he said, Americans don't discriminate;
they use the same brush for both. Sooner or later
they'll cut our legs off at the knee.

When I failed, at first, to catch his meaning,
he spun in my direction, took a deep breath
and held it until his cheeks and eyes
bulged. Then he rubbed his hands unctuously,
and in the familiar nasal accent
of Peter Lorre, whispered:

"Señor Trotsky, it pains me
to say this, but you shpick Yiddish
mit a Brooklyn accent."

8

Sometimes I see the face of my father.
Lev Bronstein, he says. Was your given name
not good enough, or are you just ashamed
of being a Jew? My racial origins
were not an issue out of the public eye,
I explained. Anti-Semitism raised its head
with that of anti-Trotskyism.

My Last Will and Testament is largely a tribute
to Natalia Sedova who, as the saying goes,
stood by me in all manner of troubles.
In fact, she stood *on* me, when necessary,
so I wouldn't run off half-cocked.
She admired my jokes more than my politics
and the one line of mine she took
for her motto was "Myself,
I am not a Trotskyite." Women
in the revolution; another chapter
yet to be written. I admired Emma Goldman
in principle—fiery, dynamic—but never enjoyed
her breathless pontificating, which smacked of rhetoric,
however sincere. Disillusioned with Soviet
politics, she retreated to Canada.
Enough said.

I prefer the working class intelligence
of *The Autobiography of Mother Jones*,
a book I could see myself translating.
Organizing coal miners in Philadelphia
and West Virginia and still active
at ninety-three when she joined
the Farm-Labour Party. Her reluctance
to dwell on adversities has sustained me
all these years, after Zinaida's suicide in Berlin,
loss of my manuscripts in the fire
that destroyed our house in Prinkipo,
the murder of Lyova in Paris,

not to mention Stalin, the rise of fascism,
et cetera, et cetera, just as it sustained me
in 1935 on the lawn at Honefoss
outside Oslo, and as I recuperated from the factions
and in-fighting that plagued our days
in France. The answer, father, is no:

I'm not ashamed to be a Jew, but often
I'm ashamed to be a man.

9

When I was a boy, Kasimir Antonovich sold me
a sack of pigeons. I crawled though his filthy attic
in the dark to catch them. Ivan Vasilyevich
helped grab them, but all hell broke loose
after we uncovered the lantern.
There were cobwebs
in my eyes and the smell of mouse droppings
filled my nostrils. All this to no avail—except,
of course, as education—since, after we'd built
our own loft and equipped it for breeders,
they all flew back to their former residence.

I'll spare you the obvious political
analogies. What if the proletariat
cannot rule, what if they fail to achieve
revolutionary consciousness? Lenin
might have found a way. His vision

was inclusive. Comrade Martov could
construct a watch that told time accurately,
but Lenin knew the laws of physics, Earth's
rotation on its axis. Axis, I should expunge
that word from my vocabulary.

I lie awake at night thinking
of my beloved Lyova, allergic to dust
and certain insect bites, found wandering
in the hospital corridors after his operation in Paris,
poisoned, delirious. He wanted nothing
to do with Mexico or chickens.

Kasimir Antonovich married a beautiful woman
but died a year later, when a bull gored him.
I imagine him thrusting another sack of pigeons
in my face and saying: Pay attention, Lev Davidovich,
everything comes home to roost.

10

I've become, by default, a chicken
psychologist. Behold my disciples,
my devoted audience!

Zinoviev here, with the clipped wings
and tilted head, was described as "panic itself"
during the siege of Petrograd. He spends
his time in blissful spasms or prostrate

on the couch, in response to reports
from the front. He'll survive, of course,
and thrive on bureaucracy.

                       Next to him,
comb bristling, is General Krasnov,
elegant but unreliable with his traitorous
alliances. Ladies, beware! He fancies
Kseshinskaya, our fancy dancer, bird
of a feather, once a favorite of the Tsar,
who hangs out with the rabbits, eating
their greens and dreaming of fur coats.

And, if I may, Larissa who, like her namesake,
flashes across the garden, a meteor, blinding
mere mortals. She was prominent in the Fifth Army,
in intelligence, then in writing brilliant sketches
about the civil war. Her career will burn
brightly, but not long.

I leave 'til last Rosa Luxemburg, whom I admire
from a distance. Sickly but noble, with eyes
that radiate intelligence. Rosa is subtle,
merciless in her assessment of ideas
and strategies. I find myself in this whirlpool
by accident, she says; I should have been tending geese
in the fields. Rosa, blessed Rosa,
who takes comfort only among the cacti.

And the egg itself? An imperfect sphere
of possibility. Obdurate, said
to be unbreakable if pressure is applied
equally at all points.

II

In the company of Jean Van Heijenoort
we took a train from Paris to Antwerp,
then sailed to Oslo. We can't seem to escape
our French connections, Van said, pointing out
the name *Paris* on the ship's bulkhead.
Our new hosts may view this ship
as a Trojan Horse, I replied.

I was thinking of the series of flip-flops
of the Norwegian Labour Government,
which granted a visa, cancelled, then
reinstated it for a six-month period.
Our reception would not be enthusiastic.
Apart from Konrad Knudsen, who gave us the use
of his house, and a few other individuals,
the Norwegians were asleep. War, revolution,
the upheavals of fascism, had washed over them
leaving not a trace. Our future consists
of hot and cold showers, I teased. They
complain only of the weather. Now
they'll have a tempest in a Russian teapot,
a circus in a samovar.

By sea we travelled more or less
incognito, thanks to émigré passports
from the Turks and the extreme barbering
I submitted to in Grenoble. The garrulous Figaro
refused, at first, to cut my hair short
as he thought it looked distinguished, professorial;
then he realized, rightly, I was trying
to disguise my identity and suggested
a Chaplin moustache.

We learned of the expulsion of pliant Enukidze,
the murder of Antipov. And news of the trials
was heating up in the press along with rumours
I had tried illegally to enter Norway
on a previous occasion. After a short reprieve,
I collapsed again from nervous exhaustion,
unable to eat, read, or think. *Rien.*

The lion, fully shaved,
but still bearded.

12

Frida? Passionate, yes, but also lame
and not exactly wasp-waisted. By the time we met,
she was spending whole days in a wheelchair
or in hot baths for relief. It's fair to say
I was taken with her wit, crude
humour, and almost primitive intelligence.

We were installed in the Blue House
in Coyoacán and spent too long in the role
of honored guests for anyone to tolerate.
My work went on, regardless. In arguments
she often took my side, infuriating Diego,
especially after his periodic absences.
The intimacy she insinuated was meant
to make him jealous. I wasn't immune
to her game: flattering an old man,
with his headaches and high blood-pressure.
I couldn't concentrate on writing
when she sat in the same room with a book.

The blow-up came when I tried to explain
the "neither war nor peace" strategy
that had guided our 1918 negotiations
with the Kaiser's minions in Brest-Litovsk.
Diego was drinking heavily and Frida,
as conspicuously as possible, placed the bottle
of tequila just beyond his reach. Natalia Sedova
had abandoned diplomacy for bed,
but the door to our room was slightly ajar,
so I knew she was not sleeping. Diego
could not be convinced the stalling tactics
had succeeded and pointed out the harsher terms
of the eventual peace agreement.
He was a good Communist, but pressure
from Stalinist trade unions to sever connections
with me was building. It's perfectly obvious,

Frida announced, turning her chair dismissively
in my direction. He grabbed her cane
and pulled the tequila towards him with the crook,
drinking straight from the bottle. Frida's
smile froze him in that position for several seconds
before the bottle shattered on the table edge.

Several chairs overturned as Diego crashed
through the house, his final curse
a faint whisper in the street. He had been
sober enough to make a linguistic distinction
between the verbs *stall* and *delay*. Peace
was delayed by fog, he said, but Trotsky
has stalled in this house for two years.

In the silence that followed, I could hear the click
of Natalia Sedova's door.

13

We'd made a sort of peace with the Americans,
whose country was born in revolution
and forged in civil war. England was another
matter altogether. After driving Yudenich
from the gates of Petrograd and back across
the Finnish border, with his foreign backing,
superior forces and advanced technology,
anti-English feeling was so intense I felt a need
to educate my troops and wrote the following memo:

> *Besides the England of profits, of violence, bribery,*
> *and blood-thirstiness, there is the England*
> *of labour, of spiritual power, of high ideals,*
> *of international solidarity. It is the base and*
> *dishonest England of stock-exchange manipulators*
> *that is fighting us. The England of labour*
> *and the people is with us.*

As War Commissar I inherited
an impossible situation. We had to substitute
improvisation for a system that did not
exist. Though I erred on the side of pedantry
my observations were basically sound.
Most of them. When one of our automobiles,
mounted with machine-guns, became stuck in mid-
stream and I cursed its low-slung engine, Puvi,
my Estonian driver, lifted his cap and said:

"I beg to state that the engineers never foresaw
we should have to sail on water."
A brick, as the English say. If only
I could see Puvi again, and my train crew,
none of whom would question my integrity
or go on and on about Kronstadt.

14

Old age is the most unexpected thing
that happens to a man.

I'm condemned, by bad health, to the reading of novels.
If Stalin doesn't kill me first, popular culture
will do the trick. No grace, no artistry,
not even an idea to burn. Confirms my view
of the English bourgeoisie as cultivated savages,
who gape at processions of royalty
and enjoy reading Edgar Wallace's novels.

I was equally disgusted by the sorcery of Lourdes,
trafficking in trinkets and miracles to scare and uplift
the little people. And the papal blessing transmitted
by radio waves—the chief Roman druid
disgracing a proud technology. How ironic
that my nickname in coded letters from Lyova
was "Crux." Trotsky, the cross contemporary history
refuses to bear; yet organ-destroying microbes
may cross the finish line first.

15

Whose is this disembodied voice I hear
on the machine talking about translation?
I'll be translated bodily. Not to heaven,
but to "a junkyard for dead materialists,"
where the parts can be recycled.

Lenin coined that phrase, I believe.
I first heard him use it in Petrograd,
in relation to the terrible waste of talent

in purges. Decades of industrial
and professional know-how sacrificed
for the fleeting pleasure of revenge.
He made a strong case for integrating
the old guard, believing re-education
would bring them round. No alternative,
really, with war on our doorstep
and chaos looming. Some of the officers
came on board to save their skins.
Professional soldiers amongst them
recognized a job needing to be done
and had no trouble switching allegiance.
Their fiefdoms were *le petit pays*
of the cruiser or battalion;
their pride, the well-oiled machine
doing its job. In extreme heat
my new toy refuses to do its job.
The quality of reproduction deteriorates
—disembodied voices can be erased
or rendered unrecognizable.

Still, I prefer to think aloud in private;
otherwise, I get distracted trying to imagine
what impact my words might be having
on the stenographer. I keep wanting to interject:
Does that make sense? Have I made myself
perfectly clear? So this is my hymn
in praise of the dicta-phone, a tribute
to Little Joseph's mechanical ear,
his unfailing memory.

16

Genuine intellectual creation is incompatible
with lies, hypocrisy, and the spirit of conformity.
Yes, there's no more than a passing reference
to the Kronstadt uprising in *My Life*. The sailors
were conned by agitators and Old Guard officers
we hadn't properly educated. They proclaimed
a "new revolution" and sent their demands
by telegraph to Moscow and Petrograd.

After some hesitation, I ordered the Red Army
to attack across the ice. Food was scarce,
the country in the grip of unseasonable cold.
It's said a man sees his own death years or decades
in advance of the event. As a child I believed
I'd be found frozen in a snow bank like the blonde
heifer, its legs tucked underneath in a vain effort
to conserve heat. Exile to Mexico's warmth
seemed a reprieve. Cognition emanates
from the intersection of nature
and consciousness. The latter serves
as a movie camera, extracting moments
from nature's continuum and presenting them to us
interrupted, in a manner that exploits the eye's
credulity. I'm echoing Vertov
and the others here. Film, where everything,
for a time, was silent, except the theorists.

The ice at Kronstadt
was red with blood that wouldn't
wash away until spring.

17

By the end of the first month of winter,
the old plugs that worked our farm
in the Ukraine resembled the drawings
of shaggy prehistoric beasts. Politicians too
hair up against the abrasions of public life,
though they aren't half so useful as draft horses
and seldom pull their weight or learn to forage
in deep snow. Stalin grew a thick skin,
surrounded himself with a protective coating
of flunkies and sycophants. Bukharin, a
perfectionist, a detail man, could not tolerate
uncertainty or compromise; he proved a liability
or worse during the siege of Petrograd.

Stalin's assassins had no difficulty locating the weak spot,
the Achilles heel, in these soon-to-be-extinct
creatures. Myself, I am blind
to the failings of those who love words, ideas;
a book or essay, sufficient passport.

Where is Frank Jacson? He looked ill
during his last visit, dehydrated, green
around the gills, and carried an old overcoat
on his arm, depositing himself rudely
on the edge of the desk as I tried to make sense
of his convoluted prose. I did not object
to this, or the un-removed hat, lest I encourage him
to stay and further interrupt the stout attack
on pacifism I was pouring in the metal ear
of Little Joseph. He took himself off
with the article, my few suggestions,
and the offer of a second consultation.

France has capitulated. And England, finally,
has something worse to endure than the novels
of Edgar Wallace, as aerial bombardment
continues. I remember Andre saying
while we talked with Diego in the garden
of the Blue House, "Surrealism will not prevent war,
but it will make an endurable peace."
From that discussion, and our collective forays
against Socialist Realism, I articulated my view
that art can be the revolution's great ally
only insofar as it remains true to itself.

I wish he were still here—Breton, that is.

I was attacked for not fraternizing,
not putting in appearances at the ballet
or giving lavish parties for my friends
and associates. Socializing—is this
what it means to be a Socialist?

Shrewd as I am said to be in terms
of theory, I lack the capacity
for intrigue. Ferocious in defense
of revolution, to quote Lenin,
yet I formed no alliances
to protect me against calumny,
or careerists. Society bores me,
though individuals may be as curious
and engaging as books. Take
Cardenas, for example. No, not
el presidente who granted me asylum.
I don't move in those circles
anymore. I mean Frida's gardener,
who'd lost a leg fighting for Zapata
near Veracruz. He confessed quite openly
his faith in vegetables. Wounded
in one of the hacienda's cultivated fields,
he'd made a tourniquet from grape vines,
then stuffed himself with tomatoes and carrots
before passing out. *I've devoted my life
to vegetables, not politics.* His brown face

a nest of furrows, yet the smile unmistakable
beneath his hat brim, squinting into sunlight
and using the shovel handle for balance
as he rolls another cigarette.

Sometimes I listen to my own voice
on the wax recording surface
and have to laugh. I have no talent
for small-talk, though I can hold forth
for hours on points of doctrine
or certain species of plant.

Don't get me started on cacti.

Cardenas's artificial leg, scrubbed
and drying by the adobe wall,
rises from its detachable
foot like an exclamation mark.

He takes the drink I offer,
raises an arm in mock salute:

¡Viva Patata!

20

Sieva, my beloved grandchild, spends too much time
in this prison, consulting with ancients
who go about their dubious affairs
under the threat of death.

He loves the rabbits as much as I do
and will not go to bed without reading to them
in German from the book of fairy tales,
his last gift from Zinaida. He'll soon
be the only Bronstein left. Safer, perhaps,
than bearing the name of Volkow,
another of Stalin's million expendable
fathers. He knows the three guards
on the street by name and asks Moreno
for leftover greens from his wife's
mother's restaurant. The attack troubled him
less than Robert's disappearance
and subsequent death.

I remarked last week how light from the gooseneck
lamp gathers about his eyebrows, knitted
in concentration. Natalia says
he "positively shines with intelligence"
and insists her assessment is devoid entirely
of the subjectivity of grandmothers.

Sieva studies the map of Mexico in my office
and already knows the regions and their capitals,
not to mention their chief agricultural
products. He learns more about rabbits
than Bolsheviks in this establishment.

21

Three weeks later, with the spring thaw,
Kronstadt would have become impregnable,
haven for every reactionary and malcontent.
So much for my sailor boys, once the pride
and glory of the revolution, who helped eliminate
Kerensky and his lackeys. Their horticultural commune,
housing committees, and talk about returning power
to the local Soviets didn't fool me. Fourteen
clandestine issues of *Izvestia*. I read every one
and watched the rhetoric grow more inflammatory
by the day. Kotlin was our only sure defense
against attack from the Gulf of Finland,
an island fortress where they were free
to conduct monster rallies in Anchor Square
and crank out counter-revolutionary propaganda
without interference. I dropped a few bombs
in their midst and warned they'd be shot
like partridges. They refused to turn over Skurikhin
from on board the battleship *Petropavlovsk*,
calling me a dictator, an evil genius,
and comparing me with Maliuta Skouratoff,
the scourge of Ivan the Terrible, and the Tsarist
General Trepoff who advised his troops
not to economize on bullets. I followed
their advice. I took nothing personally. Instead,
I took the measure of yeoman Petrichenko,
who could use metaphors to persuade;

he, not Sklovsky, was spokesman and leader
of the revolt. No ordinary seaman, he spoke
of seizing the rudder from the Communists
and sailing the re-fit Soviet vessel to Petrograd,
then to all of Russia. I had to act, being one
of the warned-against shoals. They were no fools,
even if they misspelled Yudenich. "Listen,
Trotsky," he wrote, "as long as you succeed
in escaping judgment, you can shoot innocents
like partridges, but you cannot shoot the truth."
Being called a butcher in wartime is no great insult
—no room there for weakness or hesitation—
but to be accused by a puffed-up, traitorous rating
of destroying truth. If they wanted General Trepoff,
that's what they'd get. No bullets spared.

22

I should have dismissed Jacson
for his impertinence, never mind the vacuity
and wrong-headedness of his article.
Forced, in my exile, to suffer fools and play
the teacher. No reminders of my iron fist
except an alarm button and revolver
mired in this blizzard of correspondence.

The heavy guns from Krasnaya Gorka
were enough to soften them up, while troops
and cavalry moved under cover of fog

across the ice. The first assault in white
camouflaged uniforms had been repulsed,
decimated by machine-gun fire;
those who returned were useless, dragging
frozen, blood-encrusted comrades,
half-crazy in their ragged, ghostly shrouds.

I appointed Dybenko Commissar of Kronstadt
and gave him the task of cleaning up the city.
Those partridges who escaped the massacre
of March 17th were rounded up and shot,
not one but could have lived as simply
and as well as these chickens
if he brought his needs to our attention
without challenging authority

23

Why did Robert open my door to Siqueiros
and his gang and appear to be getting into the car
of his own volition? I don't believe
he was a piece of Stalinist shit.

What's happening to my mind, my style?
I shift with such ease to a street-fighter's idiom
that would melt the wax cylinders of Little Joseph.
Sylvia tells me Jacson carries a forged
Canadian passport to avoid conscription
in Belgium. But he hasn't avoided
intellectual frostbite.

Comrades Kuzmin and Kalinin addressed the delegates
of the Provisional Revolutionary Committee
in Anchor Square in Kronstadt on March 1st,
sixteen thousand sailors, soldiers
and workers in attendance. The crowd
attacked the resolutions,
of course, but their speeches had no effect.
I might have brought the doubters
round, appealing to old loyalties,
drawing the leadership into our circle,
at least temporarily. Prisons were anathema
to those free spirits; ideas circulated
without persecution. How similar our positions
seem now, as I assume a siege mentality,
sending my paper planes across fogbound ice,
against the thunderous fusillades
from Lissy Noss.

I said to Natalia only this morning:
"What's this, we've slept another night
without being killed and you're not happy?"

24

The cactus evolved spines to keep from being
devoured and enable it to collect moisture
from arid and semi-arid environments.
This, in turn, is carried by grooves to the roots
of the plant. Even then, various species

are nearing extinction as a result of climatic change
and damage brought on by human encroachment.

I hear voices in the garden. Frank Jacson
has arrived and is making small talk
with the guards. It's not the least bit cold,
but he's wearing a hat again and still carrying
that shabby gabardine overcoat.

Lemmings and lovers. How quickly
salesmen learn to break the ice.
I see why Sylvia is smitten
by his attentions. He can't write
or keep two ideas in the air at the same time,
but he's attentive as a domestic animal.

Even the chickens are aflutter.

Six

His mute lines are but a distant flute.

—Izzat Ghazzawi

Flying Blind

1. Voyeur

Can't help it, I have my eye
on John in East Jerusalem, the way
he folds his undershirts,

places papers neatly on a chest
of drawers. I watch, indecent,
as he explores the surfaces

we occupy, memorizes
distance, lays down latitudes
of privacy. Does the mirror

see John station himself
in front? No coy expressions
of self-love, only a man

shaving his face, soap driven
before the razor like a bow-wave.
I hang about as if he were

a ruin. His blindness unclothes
me, is an unreflecting pool.
Yesterday at Dar-El Tifl

Orphanage he was a magnet,
children drawn to him
as to a fresh start,

the lame, the unloved
squinting ones, sensing an Eden
of possibility. A young girl

biting the nail of her little
finger to the quick tells him softly
in Arabic she is Lebanese.

Another dances while he plays
and sings. They don't stare
or share my fear of the blind,

the terrible blank gaze
that sees, a God's-eye,
everything there is

to see. Dark glasses
usher John's eyes to shadow,
his mask of blindness

makes me almost visible.
This T-shirt, is it white
or blue? he asks.

2. THE BEST SAMARITAN

Consider the dust. It lies
upon the tongue. Centuries
invested in a smile, olive trees
that bear the martyrs' names.

The High Priest smiles,
extends a hand in greeting.
Amram, who calls himself
a Palestinian Jew, speaks Arabic

to John, English to me, lives
in style (one could say
high style) on a mountaintop
in Nablus, ministers to a flock

of nine hundred Samaritans.
Twenty-six centuries
of documented habitation:
what do I know about pride

of place? And the intifada?
Yes, Amram explains, a building
was torched, but he phoned
Abu Amar in Tunis, was reimbursed

within days. Not so lucky
his Arab brothers, their demolished
houses lining the road uphill.
A few hours later, John and I

will promenade among the ruins
of the Temple of Augustus
at Sebastiyeh, where the Baptist's
head was served on a platter,

where Omri, Ahab, and Jeroboam
watched ivory palaces toppled
by invaders. Alexander the Great,
John Hyrcanus, and Sargon II

the Assyrian had time to kill
and axes to grind in Samaria.
Against such history, L-5,
a herniated disc and my sciatic

nerve screaming blue murder.
The blind leading the lame.
Sacrificial blood stains Amram's
hands at Passover, fingers that caress

the ancient Scroll of Pentateuch
in Nablus dial the touch-tone
phone to distant Tunis.
A shepherd leads a dozen

goats along the ancient path.
His son, on foot, keeps strays
in line with a small stick,
branch of an olive tree

for another branch of the family
claiming Abraham as father.
Bared throat, the sudden
intervention. I tried to call

home, could hear the phone
reverberate in empty
rooms. I wanted belief. No
blinding light, just something

that would endure partisan
struggles, shifts in power.
Dream on. The dead
donkey at the crossroads,

legs extending like ramrods
from the bloated carcass.
An army jeep stirs dust
not far from Jacob's Well,

where the Samaritan woman
asked for living water. I can feel
the stones recoil, hidden
springs cry out in disbelief

at road blocks, guns, free passage
still denied. And clever diplomatic
Amram serves his coffee
black and sweet.

3. MOSES AMONG THE RUSHES

I never intended to document
the lives of saints, their fingers warped
by continuous prayer, bodies

emitting an electromagnetic
hum. Disciples either, lugging
their pamphlets and self-
importance. Scanning the rushes,
I notice a stranger has co-opted
my face, my voice. I watch, appalled,
as this imposter invades the small screen.

Why do Doug and his camera crew
refuse to acknowledge the deception?
A small vehicle enters the frame
behind Izzat, backs out to a parking
spot. Izzat is telling the story
of his solitary confinement. My
impersonator asks the writer
how he smuggled out his letters.
Izzat responds like a man who feels
all value disappear from the words

he speaks. He has plenty to lose
talking to foreigners, rendering
fixed and intractable the soft glottals
that cradle his narrative. I'm touched
again by these tender epistles
to literary mentors, including Israelis,
inscribed in a minute Arabic hand
on scraps of paper, rolled in cellophane
and passed from mouth to mouth by kiss
during family visits. Extraneous
background noise. My doppelgänger

projects an irritating nasal voice
and nervous edge I might have fixed
with coaching. And Christ, he's used
that tasteless pun about kisses
with a subtext. John's lucky to be blind
in this instance. He gets an extra hour
of sleep and can replay his dream-script
while chalking up rest and REM-time
on the ravelled sleeve. The High 8,

on the other hand, is not blind enough,
relentlessly gathering detail,
knitting names, gestures, and objects
into a fictional fabric not even the ruthless
guillotine of the film editor can rectify.
There in the cutting room I'll be
dubbed, patched, excised, superfluous,
and unattractive pieces strewn underfoot,
a new creature emerging, a plastic
Frankenstein to call my own. Izzat

will have altered, too, his face
on film still ignorant of the wave
of pain set to engulf him fourteen days
after this interview, when settlers
on the rampage in a school in Ramallah
shoot and kill his son of seventeen.
So much for witness, prophecy.
The documents I smuggle out

on video cassette have aged as much
as they've distorted all I've seen.

4. FLYING BLIND

When the poet's blood
shifted hemispheres, streams
were in full flood, airports
buzzed, public statues
exposed themselves along

sunlit esplanades. Someone
in a Jerusalem suburb
was stockpiling weapons,
composing prayers. What
has this to do with a poet's

wintry demise, you rightly
inquire. Words modified again
in living guts? I have nothing
against the desert. That it is rock,
not sand, may be a matter

of remorse to certain clientele.
Not me. I'm pigging out
with John and Hisham
in a Bethlehem café.
Except for two blind Arabs

and a sighted minority
consuming chicken shish kebabs,
the place is empty. Smartly
dressed, Hisham has a Ph.D.
from the States and a job

waiting in Michigan.
Home briefly to refurbish
domestic relations. Four hands
scuttle across platters, up
the sides of glasses. Spiders,

bottom-feeders, anxious
to know what is there. We'd
disgraced ourselves at Bethlehem
University, leaving abruptly
after an hour of fake Platonic

dialogue. We were told the study
of English helps adapt, think
critically, use technology, and work
in a multicultural setting. *Merde*,
I whispered to John, too loudly;

given the Vatican support this dump gets,
does it surprise you the paper's written
by someone named Pope? My visually
challenged friends have scarfed down
most of the chicken, ordered seconds

of bread which they eat unbuttered
in the Arab fashion. Hisham,
fastidious, pays his share, makes
connections at Deheishe, the refugee
camp where he stays with parents

and equally blind brother. They
owe their condition to vitamin
deficiency, contaminated water.
Ahmad offers a typical account
of military abuse. I'm mesmerized

not by the story, but the absolute
stillness of the teller, no light
emanating from his dead eyes.
If the animus is not visible
there, where does it hang

out—in these nosey, brash,
interrogating hands? Without
benefit of higher education
or the gospel according to Carol Pope,
Ahmad relates how urine,

excrement, and blood
mingled freely in the cell,
where he could neither stand
nor lie down, how they
punched him in the kidneys

as he clung to the jeep.
A crash course. He calls it
the central experience
of his life. Prison gave meaning,
purpose, made him

part of the intifada. I think
of the two Israeli hikers
killed this week in Wadi Kelt,
throats opened. Yeats gone,
his rough beast too close

to Bethlehem for comfort.
John's so overcome
he has to leave the room.
The brothers wave as our car
descends the open-sewer

dirt track into Bethlehem
proper. O little town,
mute and doggo like language
itself before the spectre
of a twenty-first century.

5. LUCK OF THE IRISH

A day off from politics,
though my back's killing me.
No polluted villages, jailhouse

confessions. West Jerusalem
shops. And, with luck, hot
dogs, a couple of beers,

an ice cream cone. Thermal
yin-yang. My favorite
outing as a kid in Vancouver
was a trip to the dairy.
For a dime you got a huge
scoop of Arctic Ice Cream,

or half a brick for twenty-five
cents. As cooling flavours
teased my throat and made
my forehead ache, Larry Flynn
was organizing shipments
in the warehouse out back.

I'd turned seven, my mother
was dying but I did not know it
yet, and life seemed good.
My health was okay. I weighed
sixty-seven pounds, Larry's
exact weight at twice my age

when transferred to Lager IV.
Die Fir Lager, "the hospital,"
specialized in helping the sick
and handicapped shuffle off

their mortal coils. Malingerers
were infected with typhus

and rallied to join the no longer
marching saints piled high
in interconnected sheds.
To find his brother, Larry ran
from shed to shed shifting
corpses whose skin, stretched

tight as Easy-Wrap, had a
translucent hue. In response
to his calls and frantic
rummaging, an arm rose
from among the doomed,
rocked slowly back

and forth, a pale flower
or metronome, saying
Wait, 78850, I am not yet
dead. Instead of fighting
in Palestine, Larry began
a second life in Vancouver

feeding ovens in an Italian
bakery, scrubbing the killing
floor of the Alberta Meat Market,
sections for hanging, scalding,
eviscerating, chilling, cutting,
and processing. He graduated

to grinding organs and guts
for fertilizers, dog food. As I weigh
the relative merits of twenty
flavours, Larry is in the freezer
backstage at Arctic Ice Cream
arguing with his brother and friends

in management about the ethics
of changing his name from Freeman
to Flynn. He toys with a flashlight
in the dim interior of the vault,
cupping the beam in his palm,
watching the warm blood pulse

and circulate. I couldn't take
my eyes off him as he gave
his testimony to a propaganda
workshop at the art gallery
on Robson Street, twelve teenagers
intent on his body language,

apologetic tone, the amount
of water he consumed, surviving
again the ordeal that will not
be denied. Our place of meeting
was a courtroom in its previous
incarnation, raised platform,

dark wood panels still intact.
As I finish my maple-walnut
cone, a trade mission from Japan
mounts the cobbled West Jerusalem
street. Male dancers and kimonoed
women distribute glossy leaflets

in English and Hebrew. I recall
my wife's delight on discovering
the manufacturer's label
on some lingerie from Asia:
WOMEN SWEAR. I wrote a letter
from my office in the barn

trying to explain my position,
conscious of her sitting fifty
feet away in the house, reading
manuscripts. What's the point,
trying to ascribe blame? she asked.
It's over. She was wearing

the blue and white striped
kimono we'd bought at a hotel
in Tokyo, the words KIMI
RYOKAN in capital letters
on the lapel. I still loved her.
My desk occupied the contested

area between box stalls,
where Simon the appaloosa
and Chadwick the baseball donkey
had jostled for space and hay
under the old dispensation.
Predetermined banalities—

ice cream or evil. His bray
began as an asthmatic wheeze
and grew to such proportions
the horse used to quit the barn
at a gallop. A vacuum cleaner
with hiccoughs. Exhausted

by his performance, he'd lean
against the partition for support.
A hand rises from the judicial bench
to guide us. Or conduct our requiem.
If Mengele jerks his thumb towards
the bathhouse, we'll be saved.

6. EYELESS IN GAZA

Late night TV documentary
on the military occupation.
This time a personality profile
of the commanding officer,
young, toughened, presented
as someone who wants peace,

if only to get out of this hellhole
and back to Jerusalem, Tel Aviv.
No mention of Palestinians,

the 10,489 injured and dead
in Gaza in the early stages
of the intifada. Creative
bookkeeping. No budding
humanist. A career soldier
determined to keep the lid on,
suppress revolt. His outpost
commands the city, binoculars
picking up every movement

in the streets, down to the infrequent
shitting of donkeys. He keeps an eye
on equipment, the gravel-sprayer
first used on women in 1988
during a demonstration in Nablus,
and an eye on Dr. Eyad el-Sarraj
in the only medical clinic. He condones
the kidnapping of victims of military
violence to intimidate families

and destroy evidence. Tradition,
part of the great chain of command
that reaches back to Menachem Begin
who blew up a Jerusalem hotel
killing a hundred people. State

terrorism. Turn the territories
into suburbs, reduce Palestinian
nationalism to a municipal matter
regulated by ethnic councils,

folklore clubs, cultural grants. Want
to publish a book of radical poets?
Why not, but remember to acknowledge
your patrons on the copyright page.
A summer job in repertory
in Haifa, restoring the wings
of angels, where they hung
like albino bats along the south wall
of the props department. Edeet,

who smiled at his awkwardness
and thought he had promise as an actor,
left for the States after 1982
when 400,000 took to the streets
in horror at Sabra and Shatilla
and nothing changed. Annexation
carried obligations (citizenship,
suffrage, the usual abstractions),
but *autonomy*, ambivalent,

permitted settlement, gradual
displacement of the local population.
He's read the reports, including
those perpetrated by P.H.R.I.C.

and S.C.F.; better written
and at least as credible. Rami Abu
Samra, 10, shot in the head at the door
of the Sala Eddin mosque, where
he replenished the water supply

in the refrigerator, tended the garden
(the I.D.F. claimed he had thrown,
or aided in throwing, a petrol bomb).
Manal Samour, 14, shot in the chest
at Shatti Refugee Camp, not for stones
thrown, but for helping a friend
injured in the same melee. Hanada Abu
Sultan, shot in the head entering
a pharmacy with her sister, ferried

to Shifa Hospital, then Tel Hashomer
and a hurried, improvised funeral
attended by only ten relatives.
They'd be driving Mercedes by now
if they'd let us get on with the inevitable
expansion. Volkswagens, anyway.
They carry politics like disease.
Dogs licking wounds. Simcha
was wrong: there's nothing

clean about a dog's mouth. Maggots
are more efficient against infection.
What's heavier than a mother's empty

arms? You can shove those cameras
up your ass. Liberals, Sunday School
teachers. We'd be rotting still in Dachau
if we'd waited for you. *For every Jew*
that dies another angel mounts the wind,
its precious eyebrows lines of dancing fire.

FOOTNOTES

S.C.F.: Save the Children Fund

P.H.R.I.C.: Palestinian Human Rights Information Centre

I.D.F.: Israeli Defense Force

Of course, none of this is reliable, not even the poetic flourish at
the end, designed, perhaps, to draw attention away from other
more blatant biases in the text. What the television crews "or-
chestrated"—or "cooked," as we used to say in science class—has
prompted from the author an equally distorted picture. As reader,
you have to wonder what the governing mythos is in this kind of
writing, and what this sort of deliberate blindness can possibly
hope to achieve. This entry, if you haven't already noticed, is writ-
ten from an omniscient point of view, a nameless, unidentifiable
narrator purporting access to the mind of the televised version
of a military commander, whose spatial and temporal circum-
stances are so remote as to be essentially unknowable.

There is an overabundance of angels and eyes (despite
the title) in this text, implying special pleading or privileging of
the divine and the empirical. An eye for an eye, a stone for a stone,
and that dubious category, the eye-witness. All things considered,

you can't help but suspect the author, if not of outright anti-Semitism (and this for Arabs as well as Jews, both being Semitic peoples), at least of general misanthropy, perhaps attributable to an unfortunate self-hatred induced in childhood. Too long a victim himself, he now resorts to the tyranny of words to victimize others and distort reality, appropriating stories to achieve authenticity, marshalling so-called first-hand experiences in quaint personal anecdotes and sly narratives and passing them off as evidence, which any reliable historiographer will tell you is always constructed.

—The Editor

7. Buying Time

Okay, so I'm the one who's
blind, imposing my own reading
of events, of John. I close

my eyes to what I can't
accommodate. Theodor Herzl
had the same problem

during ten days in Palestine
in 1898. He noticed no Arabs,
only a mixed multitude

of beggars lining a dusty road
to observe the Kaiser's visit.
Unless he was a certifiable

villain, Herzl's blindness
was necessary to the Jewish-
Ottoman Land Company

he was trying to promote.
Meeting with Abdul Hamid
in Istanbul in 1902 to propose

his scheme for colonization,
he lied to the Sultan, pretending
friendship and offering to solve

the problem of Turkish debt.
Meanwhile Ibrahim, Grand
Master of Ceremonies, put

his own spin on events,
and Izzet al-Abed, a Syrian
serving as Court Chamberlain,

used his poker-face
and diplomatic skills to full
advantage, buying time,

imposing restrictions, faking
outrage. Back at the hotel,
after he'd declared

in a farewell letter his people's
respect and love for the august
person of the Caliph,

the only great friend we have
on Earth, Herzl sat down
to his diary and described

his hosts as *bums, a tangle*
of venomous snakes,
their leader *shabby*

and *noxious,* with big ears
and the *hooked nose*
of a Punchinello. Duplicity

protects us, writes Paul de Man,
accused of collaborating
with the Nazis, his eloquent

pen traversing the page
in the service of a formidable
intellect, an unnameable past.

Rhetoric transgresses, why
should this text be different,
my own narrative a nest

of delusions. The population
of Jews in Palestine
less than two percent in 1900,

de Rothschild's support
notwithstanding. I was searching
for something incorruptible

to translate, how we come
to depend on love, the myriad
little gestures so often

taken for granted, the way
a wrist bends and the hand
opens towards you, lines

fully exposed. Home plate.
Was first base even an option?
Hit the ball, then try to stay

mounted as they push-pull
the beast around the infield.
Lips move silently,

trying out the words. I keep
thinking, if redemption's
your game, travel by donkey.

8. Borderline Schizophrenics

What am I doing in this rented vehicle, driving John to the Lebanese border? I could be interviewing Hamas or meeting dissident Jews in Tel Aviv. Instead, I'm chauffeur to a Homeric Arab napping in the seat beside me, more at ease in his dim world than I in my troubled visible one. Yesterday we visited a hospital in East Jerusalem whose funding was cut as a result of unwise alignments in the Gulf War. Minutes into our interview, the presiding doctor excuses himself and returns with a peasant from Gaza, whose son needs immediate medical attention. The first procedure, diagnostic, is to be done by Israelis since they have the best equipment. Given positive results, treatment can begin. The bald challenge works and we part with the desired cash in traveller's cheques. The old man thanks Allah, the doctor thanks us, and we thank Nawal Halawa for setting us up. The sick child, who wants only to go home with his family to Gaza, runs screaming down the corridor when he hears the good news. The cost of playing God is modest here. Even a Jew like Bill Freedman from Chicago, who teaches poetry at Haifa University, has to moonlight to make ends meet. He's a paid shrink in the evenings, composes poems, and dreams of spending a sabbatical with his girlfriend in Montreal, earning twice as much and teaching half the hours. Metaphysician, heal thyself. John is unemployed back home, though doctored, published, and a gifted teacher. The prejudice has as much to do with blindness as with race. Here such stigmas don't exist; he's basking not only in sunlight but in two job offers, which he can't accept because of danger to wife and kids. The redemptive power of work. Bronwen, five, seeing me spend so much time at home filling blank pages with words, said, Dad, what are you going to be when you grow up? *Touché!* Maybe I'll be a soldier or a singer, an engineer or television comic. Wake up, Farouk, we're at the border, in more ways than one. Poets arise! Let trumpets sound! We'll march triumphant through the ruins of Jericho, Beirut. Twenty-two years in exile. John breathes the familiar coastal air, thrusts his arms between the iron bars of the barrier so his hands, at least, are back home in Lebanon, the same ten fingers that picked up the shiny metallic device dropped by jet fighters in a field outside his village, manna from Israel that put the sun and stars to sleep. *G'day, mates.* The blond Jewish soldier from Adelaide sweats out the noon shift. An Uzi, a cup of Coke in Styrofoam.

9. A NIGHT AT THE JERUSALEM HOTEL

A night of beer and singing
in the restaurant garden, tables set
under a canopy of vines
and creepers. John navigates
the cobbled path, the cane
with its white rubber tip

nosing flower beds. He settles
into a rattan chair, striped
watermelon shape of the lute
on his knees. We're waiting
for George, Musa, and Nader,
our principal singers and revellers.

Maxine Kaufmann expected too,
with friends from *The Other Israel*.
She protests internments, illegal
expropriations, writes articles
about Yesh Gvul, soldiers
who refuse to serve in West Bank

or Gaza. This week Maxine's
interviewing Bedouins
displaced from traditional
grazing lands in the Negev desert.
Our local friends, all graduates
of the jails and intifada. Loahez,

tortured and imprisoned at fifteen
for joining a group that promoted
Palestinian rights. Musa, hairdresser
and cut-up, who mocks nationalist
lyrics, refuses to speak of prison.
And George, a high school teacher

who loves poetry and spends evenings
with his girlfriend in the padded
cells of the Music Department
at Hebrew University, practicing scales
on the beloved's vertebrae, scoring
intricate sonatas. Nader dreamed

of engineering but his father's
death intervened. He put
his ambitions on hold, ran
the offset press in his mother's
basement. Before the ink dried
he was jailed. Lights go on

along the walls of the Old City.
At the depot next door, buses
have bedded down awaiting
the Messiah. Our guests
have come and John is tuning up
—we'll be transported yet.

10. AN EYE FOR THE LADIES

There's a legend in my family about a pianist
born blind somewhere in Glasgow
or Edinburgh. It was classical, I recall
(his repertoire, that is), but I prefer to think

he played at some small pub in Lanarkshire,
chords and melodies filtered through smoke
and small talk, that he had a glass of beer
on the ledge above his keyboard, beside a rose

the management provided, or an old lover.
As evening progressed his face would shine
like Stevie Wonder's. He'd lean into the fragrance
of that rose and remember the sweet funk

of sex, the flowery combat of nerve endings
on fire. A reasonable fantasy, even
for Presbyterians. After all, they named
their greatest poet Burns. Women, of course,

all love him, no snap judgements or false
assumptions based on appearance to sour
or complicate relations. Perhaps he smells
their heat as animals do, or hears the lonely echo

behind a voice, substrata of desire. Fingers
that caress ivory might also coax music
from tired flesh. Describe yourself, he'd say,
your skin's as soft as feathers and words

that take flight from your lips nest lovingly
in my ear. Women who can't let go abandon
notions of performance and feel their bodies
unfurl, all the Anne Gregories once comforted

by Yeats for the odds against yellow hair
finding true love. When I mention these
fantasies to John on the road to Nazareth,
before we offer a ride to two Israeli soldiers

returning from sentry duty at the Lebanese border,
he shakes with laughter, then tells me about
the woman who picked him up in Montreal
when he was twenty and the two Arabs seated

behind him on the bus, sick with jealousy and cursing
the injustice of such beauty wasted on the blind.
They never knew he understood their conversation
until he smiled and said goodbye in Arabic.

II. In which I assume, recklessly, the mantle of Augustine

This, for the record, is my
last confession. I call it quits,
bequeath to Francis and his
feathered friends my quill,

my quiddity, my *quid pro quo.*
Eyes tempted still by the world
and its forms. Corporeal light
distorts, its dangerous sweetness

makes me color-drunk; and
paintings, Lord, bold, concupiscent
in their revelation, hymn me
from devotions. Isaac, old, blind,

bestows his blessing on the wrong
son, dressed in goatskins
to simulate his hairy brother
Esau. Then Jacob in his turn

preferring Ephraim, signals
crossed, but doing, so we're told,
your will. Too much beauty
immolates, corrupts both viewer

and viewed. Sacrifice of
sight allows me to transcend
the merely visible. The quietist
weighs anchor, the anchorite

sets sail. Blindman's bluff's
a game for those in love
with shadows. The blindfold
executes its will, real

wool pulled over imaginary
peepers. The blind navigator
burns his charts and sails oblivious
in an opaque glass sphere.

12. HORSEFLY

Leghorn Joshua stands in judgement over Jerichoed walls,
breast a juggernaut, revving his reveille, brassy orchestrations
love-juicing the warm eggs. He pipes a slack-ass sun over the
un-scrubbed, un-knit brow of earth. Dew drenched, the birthed
barn inches, solemn, dayward; its animal freight shifts and groans,
lugged organs of delight. Yes yes to horse heart, consuming its
straggle-beard of hay in doorway, and the baleful doppelgänger

donkey in dismal disarray, shadowing in shirtsleeves. Swallows swoop from perch to pitchfork, perfect plagiarists glimpsing the death of song. Mouse glides, subversive, through the privileged motes, banks on absence. And I, fly-by-night, thank you O God—even as I languish in bird-beak, ontological stupor—for the undigested grain in horse shit, the sweet blood shed nightly in your honor.

HANAN

I

First night in the makeshift tent
I hardly slept. I couldn't stop
thinking of Daoud, unable
to protect himself from boots and

clubs as they dumped him, wrists
tied, in the back of the jeep. I twisted
for hours in that bruised borderland
of wakefulness, without relief.

Beds, of course, were destroyed
along with crockery. What was not ruined
by the force of the explosion was
scorched. I salvaged two aluminum pots

and a frying pan. One of the settlers
went through the rubble after the blast,
smashing appliances and anything
of a personal nature. A sack of flour,

still intact, was dumped on the floor.
I could see his shoulders droop
and body arch slightly forward at the waist
the way men do when they urinate.

2

I awoke before the neighbors arrived
with food and clothing they could spare,
but Hanan was gone, and the single blanket
with which I'd covered her. I'd been

so upset over her brother and the house
I'd more or less ignored her, offering a kiss
but little else in the way of comfort.
How do you explain something like this

to a five-year-old? For a moment I panicked,
thinking of the settler and his military
escort—a man who attributes
his rage and greed to God is capable

of anything—and the rabbi
who calls us West Bank Indians, favors
deportation, and wields his scriptures
like a scimitar. I ran crying

into the street. Nawal grabbed me
by the arm. Come, Mustafah
has found her. She's cold and a little
disoriented, but otherwise okay.

3

She'd appeared at Mustafah's door at sunrise
holding a red pencil and would eat
nothing until he gave her a piece of lined
paper, on which she reproduced letters

of the alphabet. I thanked them both
and took her back to the dozen or so tents
of the dispossessed families. She would not speak,
but sat quietly drawing circles

in the sand. Dr. el-Sarraj shook his head.
Time, he said, healing time. Take her
to visit Ali and Daoud in detention—
familiar faces. That night I watched her

slip from the tent when she thought
I was sleeping. I wanted to speak,
to run after her, but the doctor's words kept
sounding in my ears. I let her go,

put on my clothes, gathered up our blankets,
and stepped into the night air
among the shelters and scavenged objects.
You ask me where the anger is,

the outrage. Your committees thrive
on excess; so do my men. Isn't suffering
news enough? The phrase *refugees
in our own land* does cross my mind.

4

I recall an incident on the coast near Jaffa
when we walked along the shore
barefoot, Daoud twirling his sister
so her feet scribed a transient

arc in the water. Scrolls of barbed wire
had been rolled aside to permit
bathing on a narrow strip of beach.
Three soldiers were laughing

and playing cards at a makeshift table
near the concession, so they did not notice
the Orthodox youth swagger past
with his Uzi, sending a spray

of sand into the plate of olive oil
and hummus. He was not more than twelve,
Daoud's age at the time. Father and son,
seated on either side of me, tensed

to respond, but I placed a hand on Ali's
forearm and shook my head for Daoud's
benefit. The youth did not look back,
the soldiers continued with their game

of cards. Hanan, with a two-year-old's
self-absorption, was amusing herself in the shade
of a towel, where she'd buried her plastic
doll to the neck, half-clothed, in the hot sand.

5

No urgency now. Curfew
had been lifted after the arrests
and demolitions. My pulse was racing
and my insides rumbled the way

they do when I make love to Ali.
He used to laugh and tease me
about being such an animal. Light
from the full moon reflected off the walls

and few remaining windows as I turned
the corner into our street. The beauty
of it made me want to weep. I eased myself
past the shattered door-frame and several

hanging timbers, catching the material
of my hem on a protruding nail. Some plaster
and rubble had been pushed aside
where the children's bedroom once stood

facing the garden, and I could just make
out the small figure curled up
in the dust, hands folded underneath
her head. I lay down too and took her in my arms.

What Does a House Want?

A house has no unreasonable expectations
of travel or imperialist ambitions;
A house wants to stay
where it is.

A house does not demonstrate
against partition or harbor
grievances;
                    a house is a safe
haven, anchorage, place
of rest.

Shut the door on excuses
—greed, political expediency.

A house remembers
its original inhabitants, ventures
comparisons:
                    the woman
tossing her hair
on a doorstep, the man
bent over his tools and patch
of garden.

What does a house want?

Laughter, sounds
of lovemaking, to strengthen
the walls;

                    a house
wants people, a permit
to persevere.

A house has no stones
to spare; no house has ever been convicted
of a felony, unless privacy
be considered a crime in the new
dispensation.

What does a house want?

Firm joints, things on the level, water
rising in pipes.

Put out the eyes, forbid
the drama of exits,
entrances. Somewhere
in the rubble a mechanism
leaks time,
                        no place
familiar for a fly
to land
on

SEVEN

It is still, thank God, harder to tell lies in art
than in life.

—Peter Perrin

ORKNEYINGA

You don't expect them so far north,
these tenders of cabbage. Vikings
yes, their consuming lusts, sacking
the land for all it's worth,

leaving in their doleful wake
shards of oar and sail, ironic
burial mound inscriptions, runic,
crude: *This place would take*

even snooty Ingeborg down a notch
or two. Let the gray friars plant
to excess, then prune to scant
numbers; or lean on shovels, watch

sodden as squat Bay ships arrive
to take on water, provisions,
men. The storm, its latest revisions
of the coastline, reveals a hive

of underground activity.
Did Neolithic warrens house
your smoke-stained forebears, espouse
communal living? Piety

in stark relief: standing stones
are history's broken teeth. Seeds
germinate, the Armada bleeds
north in disarray, Neptune's throne

witnesses the orchestral descent
of the Kaiser's fleet. Italian
prisoners of war imagine
freedom, baroque, in the rent

veil of a painted Quonset's Sistine
grace. And you, authorial stance
eroded by impish time, chance
on cabbage, blue, crisp, cool, pristine.

SKARA BRAE

I was gathering dried dung
and driftwood for the hearth
when I saw the great tree
snagged on a string of rocks
offshore, its branches tall
as god-stones, thrust up
out of the water. My basket

safe on high ground, I shed
my skins and waded out
for a closer look. I'd spent
first light three steps
behind Yold, placing seeds
into the shallow furrows
his ard cut in the moist

earth. I made a joke
about our reversed roles
he didn't understand.
Yold is lame, the gash
on his leg from the jagged
flagstone slow to heal.
I stanched the flow of blood

with the flesh of a puffball,
then applied fermented
leaves. I admire the way
he uses his injury to justify
the afternoons inside,
away from women
and cabbages, grinding

tools from whalebone,
gannet's leg. I gather eggs
from shag and guillemot
with his sisters, lie in wait
for otter, for him. Yold, Yold,
I think, watching the seventh
wave break, you've no idea,

none. The ancients
I consulted say your eyes
will open with the solstice;
meanwhile, I bide my time,
scan the sea for secrets.
Water presses close
against my skin, insinuates

itself. Something's
in the branches that I can't
identify, half out of the water
—a longish bundle bound
with rawhide straps. I must
secure the tree, its wood
so rare and precious,

though instinct tells me
I should let it go,
that it brings death. All
migrations start with wood,
Skop says, wood enough
to build a boat. Water's
deep; my only recourse

now's to swim. What closes
on my leg as I approach,
drags me under? I struggle
hard against the lack
of air. From underneath
the tree seems full of faces,
father's, Yold's, others.

My foot tangled in weed,
submerged branches. I know
this icy lover wants me
dead. I can't give up, my
face and mouth contorted
in a grimace. My hands
thrash out, something solid

to haul myself upwards.
Fingers clamp, at last,
on what they need, legs
kick free, my head bursts
gasping into air, blue with cold,
with birthing. Objects
I thought faces only shags

lifting off into the gray
sky. I'm being towed ashore
by Yold, his sister, my arms
in a death-grip around
the infant cradled in its sack
of skin, skull the shape and
color of a puffball.

P.O.W.

He grew remote, acquired a language
I could not decipher. My airman, my high-
flyer, cryptic, hieratic, more complicated
than Linear B, or the Dresden Codex.

Demented not demotic, and no Rosetta Stone
to tap, I failed to crack his code,
its glyphs and glygers, the Dead Sea
Scroll of love I languished in. I regressed,

mute in the face of shifting vowels, lost
consonants. Tore my hair, mouthed vows,
cursed this vain enigma in his cuneiform.
Dismissed, of course, as menopause,

the rash that formed upon my belly
proof enough. And sleep, that famous
balm, exploded in my face. Other things
on his mind: war, unfinished business

in Dundee. Or was it Dunsinane? I was one
witch too many, no Orkney wood to order
wrapped as camouflage. I'd ruined his precious
furlough; the poems he'd planned to write

were out the window. I could kiss the ass
of my Italian gardener, for all he cared,
stepping into his plane. And so I did,
as well as all his other parts. One by one,

I felt my unvoiced cells rejuvenate; the itch
migrated south. I couldn't get enough
of him, his crazy grin, the ridge of dirt
beneath his nails. Even the quaint

Catholic saints he painted on his tin roof's
corrugations performed sweet ministries
—coleslaw phonemes, pasta pictographs—
till I too, earth-bound, human, got my wings.

WILDERNESS FACTOR

Isbister's gone. Six years in the skin-trade
earns a visit home. Divine accounting—
leave it to Hudson Bay. Each Sabbath year
thou shalt rest, return home via Montreal,
Orkney, bearing trade goods in excess
of 10,000 pounds, skins for fat burghers,
London's lah-dee-dahs. Two magpies
tear at the remains of a dead muskrat
on the south bank of the river, below
the stockade where canoes push off,
laden with bales amidships. He never
looks back, or turns to wave, the shapes
of his dark children already lost in fog
and river vapours. No swish of crinolines

here or carriages lined up along the quay
as on the day he steps ashore in Kirkwall,
a man of property, elder and provider.
No longer, as his name trumpets, John
of the "east homestead," he's slipped
into history, pre-booked passage a sign
of grace. Too polite to ask, his wife
can smell the wilderness that oozes
from his pores, see the treed creatures
stirring in his eyes, the ghostly trace
of dreams that curl in smoke around his pipe
and beard. She knows the blunt anchor
he lowers in her stagnant pool won't hold;
it will drift, be weighed, found wanting,

she can imagine what. Another pale child
to fill the spaces where there are no words,
no eloquence of touch. A seven-league
soul starving in its leg-hold trap
of flesh. She feels it suck the marrow
from her bones; her tidal estuary's
almost dry. But still his scheduled ship
decamps at dawn. Shadowy forms
engulf him at the rail, stretch the sheets
to full capacity. She feels the muscles
in her wrist contract to wave, but something—
is it pride?—causes her to pause. Too late,
the ship is swinging on a starboard
tack, the fog moves in, Isbister's gone.

SUBTEXT

When I first went on board
in Bremerhaven, the quarters were
cramped, the bunks narrow envelopes
you couldn't turn in. I could feel
my heart race, chest tighten.
I wanted to tear off my clothes
and run screaming from the deadly
intimacy of this space. I knew
no psychological theories

to explain my terror—trauma
in the birth canal, whatever.
I doubt they'd have consoled me,
weeping in bilge-water.
We inched between the sunken
vessels they used as barriers,
hum of the diesels scarcely
audible. I watched the muscles
twitch in Heinrich's cheek

as he leaned into the bulkhead,
a white oil-rag waterfalling
from the pocket of his blue
overalls. Click. Click. Click.
The Old Man at the scope,
his elegant hands conducting
the operation. A short blast
of power with the rudder full
to port would straighten us

out. Scrape of barnacles
on the starboard side, then
we were clear. Clear to deliver
our death-fish, ejaculate
into the belly of the English
cruiser. Highwater slack,
don't consider the casualties.
In twenty minutes the tide
would turn, current

surge through the gap. I thought
of the two cans of sauerkraut
Heinrich and I, in disguise,
had purchased the day before
in Stromness. Don't let Jerry
get a whiff of this, he said
in a Cockney accent as he quit
the store. The proprietor's laugh
blended with the tinkling bell.

How I Was Launched

Mother was a McGregor from Inverness,
a beanpole but ambitious. And tough as gorse.
She would not so much turn her head

as swivel her gaze so one eye peered at you
across the bridge of an aquiline nose.
My father was a short almost comic

figure from Exmoor whom she had met
while stationed in Orkney. She admired
the way he danced the foxtrot, swallowed

his vowels. His natural vulgarity
survived military service unscathed.
As a teenager I would nickname them

Jiggs and Maggie after the cartoon
characters, Maggie the great pretender
and social-climber, Jiggs the constant

embarrassment with his top hat, cigar,
and bad manners, always ducking
out to eateries in Boston for a snack

of corned beef and cabbage. My father
finally persuaded her to sleep with him
in the summer of 1919 in a small cottage

overlooking Scapa Flow, where the German
fleet was anchored, awaiting the results
of the Versailles talks. She was sitting

upright in bed, sheet to her shoulders
while he undressed, a cigarette in one hand.
As he stepped out of his bellbottoms

and dropped his underwear, not a bit shy
of his enthusiasm, she put her hand
over her mouth to suppress a scream.

Behind him fifty-four ships, scuttled by
defiant crews who jammed open sea-cocks
and took to the boats, were listing at odd

angles in the glittering waves. My parents
stood in the window, naked, his arm
around her hips, hers slung across his shoulders,

and watched. He flicked a benediction
of fine ash on the window sill, looked down
at his wilted submariner, and laughed.

Song of the Foreskin

Info, data, stats, when what I want
is the lean dirge of departure. Last cry
from the Stromness ship, a keening

so plaintive it moves like fog across the sea
and up the tarred pilings of the pier
into my bones. As if song might sustain

us, fill the void, stitch elegance into rags.
Margaret, siblings in steerage, left behind
to tend a childless uncle. Stark profile

in the first-class porthole as the blunt
stern of the steamer inches past, recalls
a cameo, a coin. Family secrets: photos,

files, subpoenas, restricted documents.
Fake brick siding on the shed out back
where blood leapt bright from the torn string

of a boy's foreskin. The crude fridge
wears its coiled brain on top for all to see.
Rain pisses down, a westerly drives cumulus

up the inlet. Mountains in the distance
transmogrify from green to brown to gray
of weathered cedar boards. The heart,

its mythic inheritance, ancient fuel pump
worn on the sleeve, corded and hanging
like a curse or amulet. I tried to sketch

the Abbey ruins, temples the Duncombes
constructed at Rievaulx. Neoclassical,
as out of place as they were out of scale.

I wasn't Wordsworth, not a jot of patience
with what he calls sublime. Not so Margaret's
gift, a wooden gauge my great-grandfather

carved to inscribe a cutting-line on boards.
Houses I'd not set foot in. My fingers
graze the threaded shank, the interlocking

nuts of the scriber, whose sharpened point
penetrates the callous of my thumb. Music.
Inscriptions. Tools. Ought that joins us.

Magnetic North

Midnight, my ghosts restless, demanding
answers. Scratches in the pantry. A deer-
mouse gapes at me in the flickering

candlelight, dives for cover behind the oatmeal,
tail exposed. I press the tiny rope of flesh
between thumb and forefinger, deposit it

outside, threatening violence. No good reason
for parting. We always managed. The first call
bagged two bachelors ambling awkward

up the gangway, oars extended
out behind their backs like wings.
At the foot of the garden, you paused

to wave, body truncated by the year's
runner beans. I leaned in the doorway,
throat dry, weak from anger, from fear,

stretched dome of my belly touching
the cold frame. Steam blanketed your face
in the frost, the half light. My saintly

gob. I wish I'd made peace. Lady Franklin
mounted a second expedition. By then,
I'd buried all hope. Journal pages, remains

of two men in a small dinghy. Sketches of a ship
encased in ice, hoarfrost diffusing a blue
light. Unmoved by history or the articulation

of private grief, the deer-mouse makes a dash
for loose foundation stones. Back in the beloved's arms
before I draw the night-bolt, snuff the candle.

EIGHT

And what does a bridge gather to itself if not
earth and sky?

—Martin Heidegger

An Educated Guess

There was this girl on the food-floor
at Woodwards. She was studying Fine Art
at college. I used to take my groceries

to her till and tried to chat her up. Katie,
her name was. I drove Katie to North Van
one weekend and showed her how work

was coming on the bridge, the two spans
inching closer by the hour. Very dramatic,
she said, removing my hand from beneath

her blouse. She wasn't talking about me.
Then she began to describe a painting
on the ceiling of a building in Rome,

a sort of pointing match where a whole
lot of energy crosses over between
the outstretched, almost touching index

fingers of God and Adam. Sounds to me
like the sparks in an arc welder, I ventured.
For that, she replied, you deserve a kiss.

A promising start, I thought, something
to build on. Katie read my mind. It takes
more than the laws of physics, she said.

High Steel

Might have walked the tightrope
in another life, another country.
Performance appealed, still does.

But, hey, this was Canada,
post-war, pragmatic, not given
to acrobatics. I stashed

my tights and dreams in the attic
for another generation, donned
boots and hardhat, stood in line

a few minutes, lied about my work
experience, presented a forged
reference and was hired on the spot

for bridgework. Two weeks later
I was promoted to the front-line,
connecting. Not my calling but

lofty enough. I could feel
the angels brush my shoulders
as I walked the beams.

PRELAPSARIAN MUSINGS

I snaked for three months, ate dirt
at ground level before I graduated
to setting steel. Then two weeks
on a raising crew erecting the Aussie

jumper cranes called kangaroos. Six
in all, with operator, tagline, hooker-on.
Hell, nobody likes the tagline. Gotta
keep it taut so the steel rises straight

and level. A smart-ass newcomer
makes a snag, knocks his mates
to Kingdom Come or slips the choker,
sending steel down into the hole.

But a good crew—Christ, it's ballet,
crawler hook booming down for the pick-up,
counter-weights inching backwards,
shifting the distribution. Set steel in place

and, bingo, Bob's your uncle. Connector
bungs in his bolt, Hot Wrench secures it
with a grunt and a few quick twists.
Kiss me, Julia. Sweet perfection.

I HAUNTED THE BRIDGE from pitch-black until the first rays of sunlight spilled like molten lava over the mountain peaks. In winter the earliest commuters slowed down, curious. Was this a potential suicide or just a nutcase? I pretended to be counting traffic, or recording the makes of cars into my notebook. In truth, I was erasing. So much of what I'd already written seemed useless or lame. I wasn't Sonny Rollins, playing tenor sax on the deck of the Williamsburg Bridge at daybreak, though this, too, was a sort of wood-shedding, an emptying out. I'd watch house lights come on, in the poorest areas first, a cramped hand groping for the alarm clock, feeling its way along a darkened corridor to the can, blocking out what the bare bulb revealed, mirror cracked, some of its reflecting silver chipped away. Then a child would cry, neighbor's dog bark. Fat's in the fire and we're gonna get higher, mainlining caffeine, mainlining nine to five, hell-bent for weather, boots, raincoat, lunch bucket, set of keys. Music had its uses. The musician did it for the beauty first, for shading, tonality. I was listening for the voices of men who built the bridge, the survivors and those lost. More than that, the blood that beats in language. It disappears so easily. Business, urgency, self, they destroy song as readily as they cheapen story. What, then? Something crafty that would soar and seduce, a score as mercurial as the maestro's title track, a bridging melody. The lives, the underlying stories, that add layers, accrete, build up like coral. I wasn't about to jump, not like Cooperman, his Jewish angst, his flair for the dramatic. I wanted to experience hell but come back and write about it. Skinny poems had been his trademark, verbal Giacomettis, Bergen-Belsen love-notes. I never talked to him about jazz, the concerts with Miles and Coltrane, though music might have saved his life.

OVER-EASY

We were sitting in a small café
across the street from BC Sugar.
A late lunch, several trucks lined up
for bags of hundred-pound white,

the chutes triple-waxed and fast.
We'd release the bags like rockets
zigzagging down six floors to explode
on the loading dock. Some drivers

are slow learners; others treat you
with respect. They know how fragile
the social contract gets as lunch hour
approaches. God, it was blue, the sky

a currency even the poor could bank
on. We'd ordered our usual, eggs
over-easy, with an extra side of toast,
when the first of five ambulances

shrieked past. It was difficult to imagine
disaster on such a day, the birds
singing Hallelujah on the wires, clouds
on strike, growing things amazed

by their own virtuosity, operatic,
playing the clown. The radio, having
kept its counsel, suddenly belted out
the news, interrupting a ballad

by Crosby, something about dreams
dancing. We piled into the street
and moved en masse to the waterfront,
holding our breath, daring our eyes.

GRAVITY, GRAVITAS

No warning, unless you count
vibrations, sudden shrug
before the bridge collapsed.
I felt it all right, stomach
rising to my throat. My god,
I thought, it's going down.
No time for philosophy;
no time for analysis. Simply,
I'm going to die.

The question
is not did you feel fear—of course
I felt fear—but the stages,
changes in intensity, a moment
of almost exhilaration, facing
the ultimate, a self-pitying
cringe in anticipation of pain,
the whole spectrum,
the works.

I thought of my kids,
their faces hearing the news,
my wife's hand inching across
an empty bed, my car left parked
in the employees' compound
and the Little League tournament
next weekend.

I recalled
the acceleration of gravity,
thirty-two feet per second
per second. And the graph:
velocity versus time.
Yet I might have been falling
in slow motion, given
the kaleidoscope of images.

I'd just released my tool-belt
when I hit the water.

Roots of Heaven

I was reading a novel when news came,
chapter on the massacre of elephants
at Lake Chad, hundreds machine-gunned

as they plunged into the water. Arab
poachers wanted ivory; the locals,
live specimens for the zoos. I was

stunned by the violent description
and was thinking of the strange
assortment of characters the writer

had conjured: a priest, a journalist
from the States, a French officer,
and an escaped German POW.

A cop stood in the patio, peaked cap
turning in his hands. Must have seen
panic in my eyes. Before I slid

open the glass doors he mouthed
the word *accident*. O God, not my son!
I screamed. I was that leathery

beast bellowing her pain, trunk
raking the air for the scent
of her newborn. I flung myself

amongst the roses, bloodied,
bereft. How little it takes
to sever connections: a trigger,

a saw, a miscalculation. Blood
lingered for days on the shores
of Lake Chad; here, but a few

seconds. Girders, piers, elephantine
in their grace, sweeping away all
I believed in, all I loved without a price.

MOTT

I'm under the wreckage, fighting a capricious
current, helmet smacking an impossibly bent
girder. Sounds, deafening only to me. Deep

groan of extinction as steel settles into the muck.
Bodies missing. Torch useless, can't cut metal
to release them. If anything shifts I'm a permanent

part of this jungle of twisted steel, rollercoaster
to eternity. Knife is all I need, simple surgical
procedure, if I can do it. Must mark my passage.

That scuba diver almost bought it, upended,
tank caught in debris. Easier this way, lead belt,
lead boots. Luscombe in performance mode

during dockyard training sessions. We dinosaurs
have our uses, he said, but can't get the lead out.
Memorize your lines. Life-lines. Follow them back.

Avoid a pinched hose, a torn suit. Nothing worse.
I peer out the small round windows of my private
fishbowl. A cameo performance: through the murk

five golden stars attached to the undercarriage
migrate along the twisted steel beam just inches
from my face. A cavalcade of color. Much

talk in the paper this morning about blame,
workers blaming the company, company
blaming the young engineer, an Aussie, new

on the job and too dead to argue the point.
Conveniently. Not just wet behind the ears,
Tom said, drowned, hung out to dry. Human error

the papers called it. Which human, we want
to know? A tremor of movement. O Christ,
I think, almost pissing myself before I glimpse

the eel's tail through my port window. Current
at full flood, blasting through the narrows, five knots,
knocking me into a pretzel-shaped girder.

Pressure okay. What about debris, submerged
logs? One could crush or pin me to the wreckage
until the tide changes and the whole process

reverses itself. I hang like a foetus
in this uterine brine, oxygen hose snaking out
behind, a ghostly sleek umbilicus.

Disbelief

To call me a mess would be a gross
understatement. Life goes on, they
said, as if I hadn't noticed. Go see

Marcel Marceau, the French mime.
It'll be good for you, my kids urged,
a distraction, anything to make you

laugh. The Georgia Auditorium
was packed, at least 1,800 throbbing
egos wanting to be stroked, lifted

out of themselves. I laughed sure
enough. Hysterically. The shushing
around us sounded like a fleet

of steam irons. I visualized barbells
crushing him to the stage, the sword
he swallowed, the one with the hilt

engraved in gold. And the park full
of old fogies, a dog-walker bending
to scoop but brushing it instead

into the bushes. I cheered him on
to come first in the bicycle race,
his big French heart about to burst

at the finish line. When he grew
from foetus to childhood, old age
and death, I wept openly. Nothing

was lost on me, not a single gesture
or facial expression. The twitch
of an eyebrow, the curl of a painted

lip sent me reeling. What's real,
what's imagined? Boundaries
had disappeared. I couldn't bear

to watch his high-wire tightrope
act, so I waited in the lobby. The kids,
embarrassed, said nothing. Me?

Guilt, of course, at feeling better.
Briefly. For weeks the faces
were interchangeable in dreams.

Cosmetics, the pale make-up
a death-mask. I'd been close enough
to see sweat fall from his nose

on stage. Now he was making love
to me. Marcel, I cried, Harold,
semen drying on my belly, the sad

white face a full moon above me,
solicitous, expressive in its silence,
the resounding silence of the grave.

FABRICATION

I've no use for fabricators. Mother's
mantra. She was speaking of liars,
people who make things up, a category

that included my brother and me. Steel
fabrication would never have crossed
her mind on the family pig farm

outside Moose Jaw. Sod huts, log
houses rubbing shoulders with brick
and clapboard. Foundries, forges

for Vulcan. Hellfire. Beams rolled
out according to spec shipped to us
by barge or flatbed truck, cut to size.

At least in theory. Length varied
by as much as an inch or two. We
ignored the difference, or found ways

to compensate, cutting, using plywood
shims, a form of cheating—mother's
kind—considered quite acceptable

around falsework, because temporary.
And the grillage? It had to support
the whole shebang of cranes, tracks,

advancing steel. A kerosene lamp
cast mother's shadow the length
of the kitchen. She lectured me

to no avail against high steel.
Down-to-earth, she keened, that's
the kind of folk we are. She was right,

dead right. I'd spent twenty years
knee-deep in pig shit. My pores
reeked of it. Fabrication brought me

down to earth again, minus a leg.
I made a tourniquet with my belt,
hugged the beam, then lit a fag

and thought of mother. You were
always the one for amateur theatricals,
she said to me later on the phone.

I SPENT A MORNING along the shoreline, the bridge looming overhead, bisecting the blue expanse of sky. I wanted perspective, a vantage from which to compare the size of boats, grain elevators, my puny self. I tried to ignore the discarded plastic bottles, tidal debris. The dead refused to talk. The individual ego again, its lyrical interference. You have to be some kind of magician, pulling things out of hats. Or a ventriloquist. Which would it be? My bag of tricks was empty; my hat delivered only dead birds. I could feel a pressure in my throat, a story needing to be told. Two kamikaze crows, no longer content tearing at a Chinese food container in the park, dive-bombed my head, their nest nowhere in sight. A tug passed under the bridge, its barge in tow close-hauled and low in the water. It was fighting the current in the Narrows, pulling for all it was worth. I knew the feeling. History can do that, heavy, recalcitrant, no freeboard at all.

ALICE

It was four in the morning when I rolled out of bed
for work and made my way to the bathroom.
Alice was sleeping soundly and did not even stir
when the bed creaked. I sat down to piss, too blind

to aim straight so soon after waking. I ran hot water
in the tub and scraped a safety razor over the stubble
on my chin, inspecting a couple of gross pimples
on my shoulder. That's when I noticed the writing.

I turned around but still had to read it backwards
to catch the drift. ALICE FUCKS ALEXANDER,
written in felt pen just above the shoulder blade.
I thought of going back to bed, demanding proof,

but it was getting late. Instead, I put the coffee on
and dropped some bread into the electric toaster.
There was a note taped to the shelf where the cups
are stored. It said: Copy those three words inside

the top-cord this morning when you get to work,
so we can think about them every time we cross
the bridge in the future. You'll find my nail polish
bottle in your coat pocket. I did as I was told.

Our message was safely inscribed by the time
the loci delivered the top-cord alongside the crane.
What're you smirking about? When the choker
was set, Charlie lifted the beam several inches

to check the balance. I'm sorry, Alice whispered
to me in my hospital bed. I guess our little secret
was too much for the bridge to bear. She kissed
the cotton bandage on my head and started to cry.

NINE

To whisper for that which has been lost. Not out of nostalgia, but because it is on the site of loss that hopes are born.

—John Berger

HERBALIST

Prescribe, prescribe. The sick
expect miracles, but seldom
pay bills on time. Taoists, alas,

are the worst. Purification
obligatory, never the settling
of accounts. What did I learn

in the ghastly desert, my sack-
cloth wretched and torn?
Meditation does not work

when the stomach's empty,
the muscles cold and cramped.
Sitting motionless in a dank cave,

no sensation in my feet, a spider
moving unencumbered across
my forehead, I had a brief

epiphany: a job, I was in need
of paid employment. Herbs
came first, treating my sores

with a potpourri of medicinal
plants. Aloe, eucalyptus. Hello,
said my body, coming at last

to your senses? Reassembled,
my ravaged parts acquired
wisdom, weight. I apprenticed

to an apothecary, a saintly quack
who followed his own advice
to the letter and died young.

I took over the business, widow
included. Her ministrations,
more restorative than herbs,

left me agog, a gong going off
in my extremities, an opiate
coursing the length of my mercantile

veins. And to think I might have
traded all this for gruel, for the
fiction of an afterlife.

Swimming Ginger

Two years at the ginger guild
marks a girl for life. Heads
turn when you pass by, smiles
or expressions of disgust. I take

the backstreets on my way
to work. Third Watch, no one's
out that early on Jieshen Alley
sorting gold, gems, colored

silk. Only hawkers of tripe, lung,
sheep's head, clams, udder,
dove, quail, rabbit. Several wave.
Others try to sell me produce.

Fourteen things done with ginger,
two unspeakable. I can't afford
wine on Crossroads Street or
Xu's infamous mutton stew,

but I like to watch the merchants
trading hawks and falcons, claws
slicing into leather wrist-straps.
What don't they know, these birds

of prey, fierce eyes that miss nothing?
They note my peregrinations
on the weekend, slipping from town
on my lover's wupan, hidden

under sacks, head and shoulders
nestled amongst unsold cabbages;
watch us bathe in back eddies,
couple like mink beside the river.

You taste like ginger crab, my lover
says. Though I dress like a man
and learn to hold the steering oar
hard to starboard for hauling

upriver, I know the time is brief
before my belly starts to swell
and the merciless falcons single
me out, pick up the scent.

Aubade

I spent the afternoon trying to fix
loose tiles on my roof. Halfway
up the ladder I saw the youngest
of Mr. Wei's daughters drift past

on a donkey. She stopped by
the neighbor's gate to allow
the animal a few mouthfuls
of long grass. Her bright red

bandana echoed the finely
stitched embroidery on her blouse.
As the donkey dined, the girl
leaned into the lush foliage

of the garden to sniff flowers.
I climbed a step or two higher
for a better view though my feet
were aching and my head felt

dizzy. I did not try to explain,
when I awoke in my straw bed
with a tile-sized blue bruise,
that I'd seen Youngest Daughter

emerge from the hibiscus, her
head and arms bejewelled
with butterflies, a silk scarf
of slowly moving multicolored

wings that lifted into the air
as she moved. All this happened
on an ordinary morning in June
without a flute accompaniment.

4)

Love was a subject I explored
briefly. I entered the fray
with enthusiasm. The lotus

flower welcomed me in,
left its perfume on my body.
Faint from departures, lack
of sleep, I embraced trees,

conversed with birds, domestic
beasts. While I soared aloft,
singing the beloved's praises,
my verses went downhill
fast, vague, abstract, given

to hyperbole. I was saved
by betrayal, bare backsides
in the long grass, one of them
bearing an all-too-familiar

mole. I exchanged ink-stone
and brushes for a horse,
bade the lotus adieu.

Notes

Page 15

In the mid-sixties, Charles Whitman opened fire on students and faculty from a tower at the University of Texas. What struck me at the time was the attention to detail that went into this terrible act of destruction. Then, of course, there was the shock of the family name—the Whitman clan producing both a poet and mass murderer—and recalling T.S. Eliot's lines in "The Love Song of J. Alfred Prufrock": "indeed there will be time . . . time to murder and create." Apologies for the "soft snow" in Texas; the poem needed that image and its pattern of stress. I thought of calling the poem "Charles Whitman to the Dark Tower," but that title felt too pretentious and literary and less universal, so I let the original title stand.

Page 24

"Time Out for Coca-Cola" is based on a news article about right-wing and anti-union violence in Guatemala that appeared in *The Catholic Worker* in the '70s.

Page 40

Years after writing "Jimmy's Place," I noticed that one of my favorite lines in the poem had originated in Gwendolyn MacEwen's *The T.E. Lawrence Poems*, a humbling reminder of how much we all owe to the poets we've read.

Pages 66–89

The Terracotta Army grew out of my travels in China with Adele Wiseman, Robert Kroetsch,

Alice Munro, Patrick Lane, Geoff Hancock, and Suzanne Paradis in the early '80s, not long after the death of Mao. Qin Shihuang's pottery army, designed as insurance for the imperial afterlife, still strikes me as a timeless monument to human folly and vanity. The book was awarded the Commonwealth Poetry Prize (Americas Region) and dramatized and broadcast separately by both CBC and BBC radio. It has gone into several editions, most recently from Peterloo Poets in the United Kingdom and an illustrated version from Goose Lane Editions in Canada.

Pages 93–103   I went to Chile during the final years of the Pinochet dictatorship as a guest of SECH, the Chilean Writers Association, to do readings and lectures and to conduct human rights interviews. The trip was initiated by Lake Sagaris and Pato Lanfranco, gifted artists and stalwart opponents of the regime who suffered many losses and indignities but triumphed in the end.

Page 107   While on a literary exchange with Mexican writers, I was taken by Canadian poet and diplomat Emile Martel to visit the Leon Trotsky house and museum in Coyoacán, a suburb of Mexico City, where the great Russian thinker and political leader was assassinated on orders from Joseph Stalin. Subsequent readings about Trotsky and the history of the Russian Revolution confirmed my sense of the brilliance, complexity, and contradictions of this man, particularly his struggle with the events at Kronstadt. For turning against former allies on behalf of the cause, he carried his guilt to the grave, reminding me of the Montaigne quotation so dear to W.B. Yeats: "A prince must sometimes commit a crime to save his people, but if he does so he must mourn all his life. I only hate the ones that do not mourn." Amongst my own contemporaries, far too few have mourned their crimes.

Page 143–181   I travelled to Israel, West Bank, and Gaza shortly after the signing of the Oslo Accords, with Lebanese-Canadian poet, translator, and scholar John Asfour, who lost his eyesight as a young boy when he picked up an explosive device dropped by Israeli fighter planes near the village of Aiteneet. We encountered modest optimism amongst Palestinians and progressive Israelis, although Jewish settlements continued to be built in the West Bank and Palestinian houses demolished by the IDF. Blindness, my own and that of local and world politicians, on the subject of Israeli-Palestinian conflict became a central metaphor in the writing of these poems. Now, it seems, I was even more blind than I'd imagined in believing the Israeli government and its lobbyists in the United States ever intended to make peace and give the Palestinians a viable homeland.

Page 185–201   Orkney is permeated with history: Neolithic standing-stones, subterranean villages, burial mounds; Viking castles and cathedrals, wrecks, and bloodlines dating back to the Spanish Armada; recruiting station for the Hudson's Bay Company; site of the deliberate scuppering of the German fleet in Scapa Flow after World War I; and the sinking of the *Royal Oak* in World War II during a raid by submariner Gunther Prien, which prompted the building of the Churchill Barriers. Among the Italian POWs incarcerated on Orkney, there were gardeners and artists, one of whom painted the interior of a metal Quonset hut used as a place of worship to resemble the inside of the Sistine Chapel. As my own family were northern Scots boat-builders and fishermen, Orkney was as inevitable a destination for me as it was for them and their boats.

Page 205 On June 17, 1958, when the north span of the Second Narrows Bridge in Vancouver Harbor collapsed during construction, eighteen workmen plunged to their deaths and, a day later, the treacherous currents claimed a diver. My father, a former Navy diver, always claimed to have been involved in the rescue efforts. Dominion Bridge blamed the disaster on the miscalculations of a young engineer, who died during the collapse, but the blame seems to me to rest firmly on shoddy construction practices and the failure of senior engineers and managers to properly oversee the plans and execution. I interviewed a number of survivors and imagined the stories of many others in the writing of *Falsework*. No one recalled my father.